*I didn't have time to write a short letter,
so I wrote a long one instead.*

-Mark Twain

It's time to write a letter or email
to someone who is distant.

(Fortune cookie insert)

A12 MONTHS WITHOUT YOU

Part 1

Copyright 2019 by Paul S. Doizé

All rights reserved. Printed in the United States of Amerca. No part of this book may be reproduced in any manner whatsoever without written permission except in the case of brief quotations embodied in critical articles and reviews. The events and characters in this novel are fictitious. Similarities to real people, living or deceased, are conincidental and unintended by the author.

Published by Alabaster Book Publishing
P.O. Box 401
Kernersville, North Carolina 27285
www.PublisherAlabaster.biz

Book design by
David Shaffer

Front cover photo by
Paul S. Doizé

Back cover photo by
Jose Andres

First Edition

ISBN 978-09982552-6-4

Library of Congress Control Number

2017916561

A12 MONTHS WITHOUT YOU
Part 1

PAUL S. DOIZÉ

Published by
Alabaster Book Publishing
North Carolina

Confession

It's difficult to have a one-sided conversation. I can't tell you exactly how many meals I spent alone in order for us to arrive at this moment in which you are reading this, but I do know it's far more than the number of dated entries contained in this novel. With the exception of grammatical errors, misspellings, and the characters' names, everything in the following pages is as I originally wrote while seated by myself in a booth at a local restaurant over the course of a year.

The intended recipient of these letters, 'J', is an actual person whose name is omitted throughout this work. However, I hope you won't simply regard these as letters to her but to you, as though you had been seated across from me. And now that you are seated here with me, please allow me to tell you about 'J' and her involvement in my life:

We started as coworkers at a local grocery store and eventually became friends. Aside from talking and joking with each other during our shifts, whenever our schedules permitted we would attempt to take our 30-minute "meal" together. Sometimes we would remain in the store itself, go to a nearby fast-food place, or typically dined at a Mexican restaurant located up the hill from our employer. We particularly enjoyed our lunch at the restaurant because we knew we could arrive, order, eat, and return to work in the company-allotted amount of time. I admit, I had always been intimidated to sit across from women and talk to them which 'J' was aware. But through our conversations, she helped me to overcome my fear even if some of the discussions were about her involvements with other men which later turned into her relationship with one man who then became the one to propose to her. I was romantically attracted to her but didn't want to risk ruining and losing 'our' friendship. Aside from being in love with her, she was special to me because as a man in his early 20's she had been my first and for a long time, only female friend. I particularly enjoyed her company more than anyone's due to her unique ability to make me feel happy with who I was which also allowed me to be my "true" self around her.

Eventually our lives took us to different places: I was terminated from 'our' employer and she transferred to a different location. I didn't communicate with her for months because I personally felt it would be inappropriate to have any contact with a woman whom I still loved and was also committed to another man. However, this didn't cause me to miss her any less with all of my heart. Her absence had a negative effect on me which resulted in a few days before the one-year anniversary of her engagement my sitting alone in a booth in a restaurant. I was drinking glasses of cheap beer attempting to "numb" the pain I was experiencing while also trying to "let go" of the attraction I had for her. One of the chefs from the kitchen whom I had befriended months before was having a drink at the bar after the end of his shift when he noticed me. He approached the booth and asked if he could sit down in the empty place across from where I was seated. As soon as he set his glass on the table he asked why I looked sad and I replied by telling him the entire story while he stayed silent and listened. When I was finished, he then made a simple statement: "Well, you need to f—king tell her how you feel." Convinced by his words, the next day I called her and told her how I honestly felt. When she replied, "I have to go," I concluded that was the end of our relationship and didn't expect to hear from her again.

About five months later, I was in my bedroom on the computer when I heard the doorbell. I wasn't anticipating anyone to arrive nor did my roommate mention he was having someone over. I walked across the house, opened the door, and noticed 'J' standing in the carport. After her initial greeting she said, "Let's go somewhere," and I recommended a Mexican restaurant a couple of miles away. Upon our arrival we were immediately seated in a booth referred to as *A12* by the staff. After we had ordered our entrees and were awaiting their arrival, we "caught up" with each other over chips and salsa. Fearing I may not have another chance to do so I reached across the table, took her hand in mine, looked into her eyes, and during the next few minutes told her how much I had and still loved her. Soon our meals arrived, she talked about her approaching wedding, we left the restaurant, and continued our conversation in the parking lot while standing next to our cars. Before our separate departure, I asked her for a current picture of herself since the photo I had of her was several years old. She immediately sent me a picture message which I would view on my phone and "write to" during my subsequent visits to that restaurant after requesting to be seated in or near *A12*.

A few weeks later I received an e-mail from my sister in which she informed me 'J' had gotten married the previous day. I continued to return to 'our' restaurant but this time with a pitcher of beer as my "companion." It was after one evening of attempting to once again "numb the pain" I returned to the house, found the photo I had requested of her during her previous visit, printed out a physical copy, and laminated it. This became not only the image I would write my letters to, but a source of "inspiration" for me.

I pretended to write everything to her.

'J' did reappear spontaneously in my life about a year later and we returned to 'our' restaurant but *A12* was occupied. However, we caught up with our lives, for me almost feeling like "old times" yet I felt more confident to be seated across from her. It was also during that visit I introduced her to my non de plume and revealed my endeavor of becoming a writer. And before our departure, although she was now a married woman, I reaffirmed my love to her.

Afterward, I would write to her in greeting cards which I felt were the best mediums to communicate my true feelings. Eventually my loneliness caused me to write letters to her, pretending she was seated across from me whenever I would dine alone at this restaurant. After a few years of little to no contact from her and realizing she may never receive these letters, my writing mentor Mr. Raymond Reid gave me the idea to gather them into one volume just in case she happened to reappear in my life someday.

And here we are.

Before closing this section, I would like to express my most sincere gratitude for taking time out of your life to listen to me. Thank you, 'J', with all of my heart.

For 'J', my Love

PAUL S. DOIZÉ

1/8

'J',

Yesterday while I was at this same restaurant I'm in now, I made an announcement to my sister: 'This year I'm finally going to publish my novel.' For some reason, since the new year beginning last week, that has constantly been on my mind. During every one of my shifts, I wonder when the day will arrive in which I won't have that "sinking" feeling of doing it the following day or a number of them consecutively. But what I haven't realized or been afraid to consider is how it will occur. Without having anything actually written and published, how do you expect to be published or even contacted? I have been making the mistake of avoiding these questions and relying on the opportunity simply happening one day. Can I honestly convince myself a letter will arrive, a phone call will be made, or someone will tell me in person they are interested in my writing? How close am I really to achieving that goal? Am I concerned about the steps following the completion of the novel? Do the tasks ahead of me sound complicated? Am I worried about failing and feeling as though I've wasted all the time I've devoted to this? What if nothing becomes of this endeavor and I end up having to work in an office, cubicle, or continue to do so from behind a counter? What about the time I lost from pursuing a career within my field of study and the chances of a better job I passed over in order to follow my passion? Have I made the sacrifices, devoted the effort, written enough, and endured what I'm supposed to in order to at least have anything even adequate or worthy of being read by anyone? Would anyone be interested in what I have to say? What if I've misread all the signs, convinced the Lord had set them for me, when during this entire journey I was traveling down the wrong road, unable to turn around and trod down another, one in which I have to settle for a lot less and having missed out on better opportunities I should have taken then? What if I've been foolish and wasted these past few years? Could I handle the regret?

Could I still regard myself as a writer?

'J',

I skipped having lunch at the store purposely yesterday so I could save the money from it and put it toward a bigger meal at the restaurant later. My shift ended a few minutes after six o'clock which then allowed me to purchase a lottery ticket for last night's drawing. During my return to the house, several vehicles consisting of police cruisers, a fire truck and "bucket" trucks had closed part of the corner where I needed to make a right turn to one of the main roads which leads to the cul-de-sac. I ended up having to cut through the gas station parking lot wondering if one of the cruisers would attempt to intercept me for going where I wasn't permitted.

Returning to the house, I assumed at most I'd be there an hour and then return near the store to a restaurant for a full dinner. After I had cleaned myself of the filth from the department and changing into my house attire, I decided to see what had occurred in the world today. About a few moments before, all of the lights in my bedroom went dark. Immediately, I cursed myself for not having paid the electric bill.

Upon looking outside, I noticed the entire neighborhood was dark. At first, I thought about reading from my e-reader by the light of the flashlight I had and then go to dinner early, providing me additional time to eat and write. But then I thought about my elderly neighbor and wondered if she was okay. I attempted to call her house and then remembered her land line ran on electricity and I was unsure if she had a cell phone. Fearing the worst, I put on my jacket and ran across the street in what appeared to be the darkest night I'd seen in awhile, my simple three-LED-bulbed flashlight being the only source of illumination cutting through the darkness. Approaching her house, I heard a chirping sound which I assumed was her security system not having any power. Running up the concrete steps to the front door, I knocked on the large glass window and was greeted by my neighbor in her bathrobe. She invited me inside for the next few minutes and while speaking to one of her sons on an emergency cell phone, we were able to silence the chirping by unplugging the battery. Once we had some quiet, we sat in the living room talking, a battery-powered camping lamp sitting on the fireplace stoop, her cat resting on the floor. We spoke until the power was restored at about 9:15 to 9:20 at which point I reconnected the battery to the security/emergency system and then departed. She expressed her gratitude for everything I had done which caused me to feel as though I had made the right choice to remain with her rather than go to dinner. I ended up eating a sandwich and some leftovers at the house, comforted by the warmth I had felt being in that partially-illuminated room with her, guarding her from whatever terrors may be awaiting outside to take advantage of an elderly woman, knowing I had to do something selfless even if it deprived me of a meal I had anticipated for several hours. I wasn't expecting any form of reward, gift, or an acknowledgment of gratitude – I just felt it was the right thing to do. That's probably why this meal I ate this evening tasted better.

Those two hours will be a nice memory to return to in the future, reminding me I can be a good person, even if some people say and/or think otherwise.

Thanks, 'J', for inspiring me to do this for her.

2/6

'J',

I was only a few seconds late from being able to sit in 'our' booth. A couple who arrived in a white luxury car are seated there, he in my place and she in yours. I was sat at the table across from them and able to see them out of the corner of my left eye. That's my life, huh? Too late to have the things I want.

I was lying in my bed with the cat before I arrived here. I was drifting in and out of consciousness as I was awaiting for the ibuprofen to take effect and disguise my pain. I had to spend some time on my massage mat to reduce the aches appearing in my back and shoulder. It was moments like those I wish I would have had someone to press their fingers onto my spine and to rub my shoulders instead of having to settle for a machine to do it. There's also something "erogenous" about the experience if the act was done by a woman whom I love and of course I would feel obligated to return the favor.

I skipped lunch again in order to put the money I would have spent on a better and more filling meal. Instead of eating in the store's lounge, I had a snack while reading a book in the small room where our food steamer is located. After the past few hours, I needed some time alone, to be in a quiet place where I could be myself for a few minutes. I could barely complete any of my tasks without being interrupted by the manager informing me of something else needing to be filled on the shelf at that second, required to answer a question from a customer, or having to stop what I was doing and have a conversation with them. Don't get me wrong, I enjoy some of their interactions, particularly those with Mr. R and his feedback from the letter I asked him to proofread for me. But there are several people who want to speak with me for several minutes and if it lasts longer than 10 minutes then I start to become concerned my supervisors are watching and wondering when I will return to work. With this new "system" we're supposed to "engage" with them as long as it takes to satisfy them which then causes us to lag in our duties with some of the chores not being accomplished. The department ends up behind, product isn't restocked, cleaning isn't done, and the "closer" is then responsible for doing everything not done earlier. And that isn't something I don't like being done to me or putting the burden on one of my coworkers. It's not fair to them.

The more of these books I read in the genre, the more I've been learning about myself. 'J', I realize I have more in common with these people than I do with any other group. What I say and think when I'm not at the store aligns with what these authors are telling me upon their reflections of their career. Their words have led me to arrive at a comforting conclusion:

I was and am meant to be a writer.

The stories they share, the eccentricities they seem to display, the realizations they have made, even the manner in which they communicate their thoughts is similar with my own. I had often wondered where it is I "fit" and what it is I'm to do with the talents, the emotions, and the mind I've been given. I can't tell you how incredible it feels to finally find a group of people with whom I belong, almost like falling in love immediately with someone upon meeting them for the first time. Or it could be that random moment when you look at them in their eyes, notice everything which you have in common with them, and discover you want to always be with that person, never to be deprived of their presence, feeling incomplete without them, as I do for you now, *mi amor. ¿Dónde estás esta noche? ¿Cuándo voy a verte de nuevo?* Have you thought about me? Will I ever be able to tell you again in person how I still feel about you? Will my words frighten you again although they are only meant to express what it is in my heart? Is that why I haven't seen nor heard from you in so long? Have you had to force yourself to forget about me in order to remain faithful to your husband? Did I tempt you to commit infidelity? Were you afraid if you had acted on the impulse, you would be ruining the commitment you had made to your husband? Do you wonder about what you could have done that day? Did you mean what you told me before your departure?

2/14

'J',

Before the day ends, I wanted to say a few things I couldn't include in your card:
    I missed you today, more so than any other in a long time. I was prepared for your arrival, hoping you would appear at my door again. Had you shown, I wanted to tell you how much I still love you with all of my heart. Once again, I reaffirm what I said to you four years ago, 'I love you, 'J', and I always have. I would marry you tomorrow if possible without any hesitation.' Adding to it, I would also want you to be my first, the person with whom I express my love physically, our bodies becoming one, caressing your soft skin, feeling your warm breath on my face, showing you passionately how much I adore you while looking into your satisfying eyes. You are whom I would want to be with, you who inspires me to become a better person, you who completes me. I realize and attempt to forget it has been awhile since we've spoken, longer we've seen each other but to me it still feels like yesterday when I said those words to you.
    Even though you are a married woman, as my neighbor

described earlier as you being "tooken," I still care for you. Although you probably don't remember me and in your mind I am long forgotten, you have always been with me, particularly during the difficult times, and have helped me to endure. It is also because of you I've tried to become a person who cherishes the people in my life who have influenced me to improve the good qualities which have always existed but were either ignored or well hidden. You also helped me to be unafraid of expressing how I feel, whether it's toward other people or myself, I can be open and not regard affection as a vulnerability or as a weakness of which to be ashamed.

I hope I haven't made you feel uncomfortable being unable to "live up" to these, but these words are the truth. I wish you were with me this evening, wrapped in each other's arms, and watching the snow as it falls. We did have the chance to walk in the snow together, remember? If I could return to that moment, I would have looked at you, dusted the ice from your face, leaned in, closed my eyes, and touched my warm lips onto yours while hoping the evening would never end.

With all of my deepest love, affection, and devotion,
'P'

2/20

'J',

Unfortunately I wasn't able to sit in 'our' booth this evening. Although I didn't have to "close," I was hoping my early arrival here would allow me to sit there. It's surprising to see it so busy here; I'm used to it being slow and not as crowded. Upon my arrival, I was seated in a booth in the other section of the restaurant. I looked around at the other diners and thought I saw you. However, it turned out to be a girl probably in her early teens. Remarkably, she appears as you did when you were 19 years old, especially with her hair as long and flowing at it was then.

My dinner has arrived and since I didn't purchase a meal at the store during my lunch, I instead bought myself a nice dinner: chicken fajitas. While I'm eating, I would like to discuss a dilemma on my mind. My supervisor mentioned the son of our DM (district manager) has recently become a "department trainer." Let me first tell you who is involved – first we have the DM who is, as you've probably guessed, is above the store manager. This DM has a son who is in his early 20's and is a department manager. Recently, the son was transferred from a recently-renovated store to one having higher volume and better sales. The same-area department manager at another store just lost his assistant and has now been transferred to another store to be trained to become a department manager. Guess who will be training him? The DM's son who was promoted to department trainer, a slightly higher position which probably also entitles him to a pay increase. The DM's son is also provided more hours to run his department, a lot more than we receive and are sometimes forced to cut. From what I also heard, the DM's son, who has been a department manager for barely a year, isn't always present to run the department. I can't imagine what the store manager over there is having to endure, with the DM over him/her and the son underneath. It probably puts him/her in a constant uncomfortable and stressful situation.

 I work hard and do whatever I am able to make our department operate smoothly and cause our customers to return weekly. I am overqualified for my position, having a lot of experience in retail along with a college degree. We, as a store, are being asked to increase our productivity while also having our allotted department hours cut while expected to maintain the appearance of the department, increase our sales, reduce our "shrink," and adhere to the rules of the company. I don't mind putting a little more effort into my job while also remaining friendly, under the assumption of what I do will be noticed by someone who is empowered to promote me or transfer me to a position which will utilize my knowledge and creativity. But what I described regarding the DM's son is unfair, isn't it? Doesn't it seem wrong this young man is being provided with an unfair advantage because of his father and the title he has? I do whatever I am able in the hope, at some point, a job will become available. But if the DM is involved, can I rely on him to endorse me or at least consider me for it over another member of his family? I can't understand why the company would allow this to happen, even permit it. Doesn't it seem suspicious a man, who probably doesn't have as much experience as other department managers in the district is given this position, probably by his father? Isn't it an abuse of his power, being able to make decisions such as these financially impacting the firm? If he's doing this, how does it look to those who would want to ascend within the company yet are only to do so if they are "connected" with someone who is empowered to do so? The whole situation sounds rigged, while this young man is cheating his way up, more than likely undeserving of whatever he's acquired. I'm not jealous of him compared to where I am—I'm upset no matter what I do to impress management and continue to be a good employee, it won't matter if there is nothing to work toward. Would you want to work for a company doing this?

Now here is my problem: I want to report this to HR (Human Resources). I realize what I'm risking – my job and potential career with them – but upon hearing about this situation, I don't care. I've been wanting to leave for awhile but I also was hoping a position would become available. My coworker in another department met the CEO of the firm last year who said he would help him acquire a job higher in the company. My coworker still works at the store and hasn't been offered anything, even with the CEO's involvement. He's been looking outside of the firm and we've kind of become "partners" supporting and helping each other to emancipate ourselves from this apparently corrupt place. As I've concluded, if you're not one of "the boys" there's no possibility of your efforts catching the attention of anyone in charge to do anything to help you escalate. I applied for a position two months ago and still haven't received a response. I submitted some of my ideas to the company for review about four months ago, and well, you can probably figure out the rest.

I don't like when someone receives an advantage because of to whom they're related. I know my father would never do anything like this to help me, even if it helped me to keep my job. Why should this man be entitled to such assistance and what gives the DM the right to do this? Isn't it a conflict of interest? Is it me or does this sound unethical? And what will occur when I report this? Will anyone be investigated and questioned? What if the HR manager and the DM are "buddies?" Will the HR manager do anything or will he/she ignore me? What if I'm accused of insubordination or attempting to interrupt operations? What if they decide to retaliate against me if the DM or his son are disciplined? Would the DM have the power to do so? What if what I heard is wrong yet I'm falsely accusing innocent people of wrongdoing? 'J', I can't continue to work as I do knowing this. I have to do something or else it will bother me during my shifts. I'm tired of my increased efforts being overlooked while someone else is receiving special treatment from people because of "who his daddy happens to be." As I think about this, we've seen this before with the LP's (Loss Prevention's) daughter, remember? I think I was too afraid to say or do anything to her while she worked in my department. It didn't really matter because she wasn't there long, but it bothers me when some people have it better because of their connections. I never received such help and was taught by my father to "work hard, be loyal, be reliable, and don't kiss anyone's a-- to get where you want to be." I'm tired of having to just accept all of these circumstances which are beyond my control and are impossible to change. An opportunity such as this, to stand up and fight for an injustice, doesn't become available often. Perhaps this is the chance I've been waiting for. Maybe this is what I've been preparing for: to stand up for what is right even if it puts a target on me. I can't continue to be a "victim" to this type of treatment, preventing me or anyone deserving of it to remain where we are, overqualified and having more than enough experience to be able to be promoted to a position not only which will improve the company, but gives my coworkers and I some reassurance that hard work, sacrifice, and effectiveness still lead to reward. Thank you for listening, my Love. I know what I have to do.

    God be with me, please.

A 12 MONTHS WITHOUT YOU   Part 1

2/27

Hello my Love,

I was unable to be seated in 'our' booth this evening. I arrived here early not only because I was hungry (I only ate two cookies for lunch) but because I wanted more time to write. And moreover, when I arrived here after my shift a few weeks ago at around 10 o'clock, I had a feeling they wanted me to leave. My sister has just contacted me and told me she and my nephew will be joining me here shortly. I considered telling her I'd prefer to be alone, and since she doesn't have to discipline my niece because she is with her father, perhaps my sibling and I will be able to have a conversation uninterrupted by her daughter's misconduct. So I apologize in advance if my words sound hurried and brief.

My sister and nephew just left and I think I'm the only person remaining in this section. I walked to the restroom near the entrance where I could see who remained in this restaurant. I was glad to see one of my of my coworkers with his girlfriend and another coworker from his second job. I made a quip about how our manger was being a "prick" today and my coworker's response was , "He always is." I can't tell you how close I was to having a chat with this man who is putting the store in danger of losing our customers, the ones I've worked hard to retain. Sounds familiar, doesn't it? But the most unusual part about this is for the first time in my career in retail, I'm older than my store manager.

I'm not trying to say I'm intimidated by this or concerned because of my age when compared to his and also the position he has achieved. Given his style of management and the response from my coworkers throughout the store, he isn't well liked and trusted. We've actually been creating nicknames for him in private which coincidentally, our collective dislike for him has made us more personable with each other. I'm not sure it's smart if he's doing this intentionally, but his manner of giving us orders and then walking away without assisting is making him appear as an a--hole who is full of himself, a common trait I've noticed in managers and the DM whom I'm hoping will be investigated and disciplined. I don't want you to think I'm intentionally targeting this man, but his recent actions, especially involving his son, deserve attention.

3/12

Hello my Love,

I wasn't able to sit in 'our' booth this evening or one connected to it. I was seated at one in the back of the restaurant in the corner near a painting of a *vaquero* lifting his hat to acknowledge a *señorita* walking next to him while he rides his horse. Another woman is near the bank of the river in the background perhaps doing her laundry. This lady has her head turned to look at the couple with an expression as though she is saddened by what she sees. I empathize with her, know how she feels, wish I could walk up to her, kneel down, look into her eyes, and speak to her. I am relieved by the painting to the left of this one in which another *señorita* resembling the one on the riverbank (although with a different hairstyle) is being serenaded by a *mariachi* playing the guitar. Perhaps he also noticed how beautiful she is and was afraid to approach her due to being unable to find a way to begin a conversation with her so he decided to convey his love for her through the only medium comfortable to him: by singing and playing his guitar. He probably noticed her from afar in the initial painting from a viewpoint not seen on the canvas. He has been attracted to her for a long time but was always too afraid to say anything. What hurt his self confidence was noticing the woman looking at the *vaquero*, assuming she wishes she was with him because of him being tall, handsome, sitting in a decorated saddle on a horse doing a dangerous job but also held in high regard by the young women of the village. They realize there are only a few of these men who have this profession, having an almost "celebrity" status. Meanwhile, the *mariachi* feels as though he isn't good enough for her because of him not owning a horse, considers himself unattractive, and works a job the inhabitants of the village feel as though he has no direction, will be unable to attract a wife due to his low income, and never achieve anything better, enough to make a comfortable living and provide the same for his spouse. His parents worry about him because of the obsession he has with playing the guitar even though he is capable of a lot more. His mustache makes him look silly due to its design and the bandana he wears around his neck may look feminine, but he has reasons for his outward appearance – his mustache makes him feel like a musician and the bandana purposely matches the color of the ribbons at the end of her ponytails, skirt, and lips: red. Whenever he sees that color, he immediately thinks of her, his mood is lifted, and he doesn't feel as lonely. He continues to perform because of how content the action causes him to be, as though it comes naturally to him, almost like falling in love. The income he earns may be low, almost on the borderline of survival and poverty, but it's enough for him to live in order to do what he loves. Although he has to labor more and spend most of his time alone in order to write new songs, it makes him happy to have such a passion where he can be creative. The *vaquero* does work hard, is usually part of a team, and makes a decent living, but his job is unfulfilling, soul crushing, and leaves him feeling "empty." Although the *señoritas* in the village swoon over him and are more than willing to "throw themselves" at him, the woman by the river desires more in a *señor*, one who is unique, passionate, and has a kind heart. She is friends with the *mariachi*, is somewhat attracted to him, but is afraid to ruin the relationship they have. She does enjoy the music he creates but she also likes the ruggedness and confidence of the *vaquero*. She realizes she is pretty enough to be with him but is afraid of whether or not he will be loyal to her, especially with the temptation of the prettier *señoritas* with whom he could easily spend the night.

However, one evening, the *mariachi* couldn't contain his attraction to her anymore and decided to take a risk. He grabbed his guitar, noticed her resting on the sill of her opened-bedroom window, and began to play a song. She was shocked to see him, surprised by the words he sang to her, and began to stare at him. He then slowly approached her while playing and singing to the point he was close to her, enough to notice her eyes narrow with a look of content relief as she fell in love with him too. He had revealed his secret, she was made aware of it, and she shared his love for him. And she continued to listen to his words, almost lost to the rest of the world while he passionately serenaded her.

Buenas noches, mi amor.

3/19

Hello my Love,

U nfortunately again 'our' booth was occupied and again I was sat in the corner near the two paintings which I had written about last week. I would still like to walk up to the woman kneeling near the river and start speaking to her in the little Spanish I can recall. Across from me in a booth to my left is a trio of people consisting of two men and one woman. They are obnoxiously loud, demanding, and are distracting me, so I apologize if my words may sound somewhat off. The only redeeming quality I notice is the cap one of them is wearing has the symbol of a character whose movie I recently watched in the theater twice. Their conversation is loud, their accents indicating from where they originate, their word usage typical of their group. I almost feel like an anthropologist observing them from afar while I take notes on their behavior. Given the way in which they're acting, I almost feel as though I'm watching animals at the zoo instead of people. Last week, two couples about my age were seated there and upon their departure, I learned a new Spanish word to describe such people: *culero*, a term appearing in my mind a few times this week when encountering those who deserve such a label. In this case, that word wouldn't be suitable for this trio and the only one I can think of is *cuello rojo*. It's people such as these with their vulgarity, loudness, lack of consideration for others around them, and overall rudeness which causes me to dislike these people enough to no longer have the desire to interact with them. Most of this section of the restaurant is empty which is causing their voices to be heard better, their conversation reminding me of a "bug zapper" - alluring because of the information they might possess but when I begin to listen, the topic they're discussing "shocks" me. I'm almost tempted to stand up, walk over to their booth, and say, 'You make the people who reside here look ignorant, as though they never learned how to speak English properly, pronouncing their words lazily as if they have no regard for how they sound around others.'

They just left and thankfully it's quiet again. I apologize for my rant, but I suppose I'm upset about our co-manager leaving. His replacement will start on Monday and from what I hear today, he worked for the same retailer as our manager and also just completed his training. As one of my coworkers put it, "Now we'll have two people who don't know what they're doing." Honestly, I was somewhat hoping I would be asked if I would be interested in the position. Given the "shark or a--hole" conclusion a coworker and I made yesterday about moving up in the company, I doubt the idea was even made. And if I had been approached, I wouldn't feel comfortable accepting it, not only because I would be in a supervisory position over people with whom I currently work, but its availability would have been caused by the manager's dishonesty, abuse of his position, and manipulation of information in order to get what he wanted. One of my customers, Mr. R, even shared his disapproval of the situation, conveying it to me in some "choice" words I'm not accustomed to hearing from him. Similar to my situation almost five years ago, I hope the Lord will have witnessed this atrocity, take pity on my co-manager, and provide him with a better opportunity. From what he told me earlier, he may be up for two possible jobs, one with a company which may move him to the Midwest but beforehand send him to a week's worth of training. It sounds as though it would be a position he would enjoy, a retailer compensating him well and provide him with the benefits he deserves, especially after this debacle. I pray it works out for him and someday it will work out for me, hopefully involving the story I "confessed" to him earlier.

Thank you for listening, my Love. My thoughts are of and with you. *Buenos noches.*

3/23

Hello my Love,

I just finished writing a letter to you in your birthday card which I sadly will be unable to give to you today. I hope someday I will be able to present it to you in person or, if something should render me incapacitated or prevent me from doing so, it will be delivered to you by a member of my family, more than likely my sister because of her knowing how much I cared about you.

    I feel very fortunate to be seated in 'our' booth right now, especially since it has been several weeks since I've sat here because it is always occupied. I wanted to be inspired while I wrote a letter in your card, looking at the place where you sat that day, pretending you are there, looking at me with your gorgeous eyes and a kind smile on your face.

    The card had a limited amount of space for me to write which for me wasn't enough even when I made and additional page on the back. Out of caution for your husband finding it and the repercussions it may have on your relationship with him, please regard this and the following words as an addendum to what was in your card and as to what it was I really wanted to say:

This evening before my arrival here, I attended Mass at my Church. I haven't been able to attend on a weekday in awhile because of my work schedule in order to have dinner with my sister and/or niece and/or nephew or because I wanted to avoid going. If I did the latter, I would spend the 30 minutes I would be in Church meditating and praying. For half an hour I would sit in my bedroom, close my eyes, clear my mind, say a decade of the Rosary, and clear my mind in order to go to my "place of serenity." Given what day it was, I felt the need to attend Service, particularly to say a special prayer for you.

There is a display at the back of the Church containing four rows of candles. In front of each candle is a button when pushed, lights the candle, a flame appearing inside the bulb. Below the candles is a slot and above the slot is a single word stamped into the metal of the display: "Offerings." A kneeler is located next to it, and on the kneeler a flat surface is on the top which contains instructions as to what to do, the significance of the candles, and a prayer to be said when a candle is lit. I visited this display, inserted a monetary offering, pushed a button, knelt down on the pad needing to be repaired, spoke the prayer on the bench in my mind, and prayed for you. I asked the Lord to watch over you today, to make sure you have a good birthday, and to protect you wherever you are. But I have a confession to make: I actually pray for you everyday, saying almost the exact same prayer, except the part about your birthday. Sometimes I'll add more to it depending on how I feel but I always ask the Lord to take care of you. My hope is God has been in your life and done whatever is within His power to keep you safe. I ask Him again, particularly on this day, as an intention I bring before the Lord, to be with you. I just wish I could say this to you in person, sitting in this booth, looking at you, and holding your hand. 'J', I still love you with all of my heart, which I almost told your mother yesterday when she happened to be at my store. But I'd rather tell you myself, again, in person.

I thank the Lord for you, 'J', for your creation, your encounter with me, and the effect you have had on me emotionally, intellectually, and creatively.

Happy Birthday, my Love.

3/29

Hello my Love,

'You had your chance.'
Someday I hope to say this to someone, preferably to my employer or one to whom I applied. I am still upset at the local newspaper paper for not hiring me, let alone unresponsive to my e-mails for application. All I asked was for the opportunity to be a reporter/photographer for them, following in the steps of a couple of my favorite authors. Given their success, it seemed logical to adhere as close as possible to their career paths. Their jobs not only allowed them to earn the finances they needed to survive, but to at least do "something" close to their passion.

3/31

Hello my Love,

Unfortunately I wasn't able to sit in 'our' booth again. Coincidentally there is a man seated in my place while the other side remains empty. I feel somewhat sorry for him, but then again, I'm here alone as well. I was looking forward to having a steak I took out of my freezer earlier, but I was also hoping my sister would call me and want to meet somewhere. She did about an hour ago and not having heard from her, I contacted her a few minutes ago to check and see if she and my nephew would still be rendezvousing at our restaurant. Sadly she informed me she would be unable to, and, because of it raining they would be returning to their house. Of course I was disappointed and not having the items I wanted for my meal at the house, I decided to go to the restaurant anyway. I realize I could have gone to the store to get the items to include in my meal, but after my shift yesterday, I preferred to stay away, at least for a day. Soon it will be 24 hours since I've been there; I'd rather not think about tomorrow's shift and the questions I may have to answer relating to yesterday. The hostess seated me in the booth closest to the kitchen where I am facing a large framed photograph of a variety of Mexican foods. I am having to sit almost on the edge of the cushion because they anchored the tables to the wall and two men with local accents are dining behind me, preventing me from moving the seat toward the table. I'd almost settle for a "booster" seat should they be available but I don't feel it's necessary. Given the amount of noise coming from the kitchen, they should give anyone who is here a discount or a free appetizer. Maybe they should make that mandatory nationwide; I doubt there would be any protests from customers who are typically seated in these areas. I spent most of the remainder of the day, after I returned to the house from breakfast, working on a model kit while watching episodes of a TV show online. Given my stress yesterday, I just wanted to enjoy my time away from that place. I opened the two windows in my bedroom in order to allow some fresh air inside while having ventilation for the fumes from the epoxy I was using. Because I was so full from the meal I had at the diner, wanting to save some money and attempting to lose weight, I skipped lunch and only have had a mug of tea since noon. While I was writing, the two men behind me departed and I was able to move the cushion forward. I am still having to lean forward which has caused my shirt to tighten. I had considered a dessert to "lift my spirits," but I have a feeling, due to the emptiness of this section, the staff will want to leave as soon as the restaurant closes. I wouldn't want them to have to remain here longer on my account; they may prohibit me from writing here anymore.

 I realize I could have spent some part of the day working on my novel, but honestly, 'J', I'm scared but more so, empty. I motivate myself by thinking the sooner I complete it, the sooner I can be free of my employer and show them they underestimated me, the DM (district manager) regarding the store manager as his "golden boy" while I possess more education, experience, and knowledge than him. My Love, I look at your photo, those beautiful eyes watching me, your smile appearing as though you're content listening to me, the hair relaxing on your shoulder and flowing down your chest. Yet I am still hesitant to continue the story because, simply put, my muse isn't physically here to inspire me. I attempted to not anticipate your arrival, hoping you would do so at any moment. I still missed you while trying to avoid making myself sad, however I wish you were here. I've convinced myself if we should ever have the opportunity to dine at this place again, I would ask you would do the majority, if not all, of the talking. There are so many questions I'd like to ask and answers I'd like to know, but I would gladly remain mute throughout the meal if it meant I could hear your sweet voice. Even if it meant you talking about your husband, the physical relations you both had, the items he purchased for you, and the vacations you both went on...I now take for granted those lunches we took while we were both working at the store and I was listening to how excited you were to be with him, what you and he had "done the night before," and eventually how excited you were about your upcoming wedding. You have already been made aware I was in love with you during that time but I had to remind myself you still regarded me as a friend and one you appeared to need at the time. I felt dishonest for deceiving you then and still do at this moment, and if it were possible, I would return to any of those conversations while seated across from you and tell you the truth, just as I did about a month before your wedding. But we both know it isn't possible and I may have lost your friendship if I had admitted it during any of those lunches. I cherished 'our' relationship, although it wasn't to the extent I wanted and I didn't want to risk losing it. I was selfish for making that determination and hope I can ask your forgiveness should the Lord cause our paths to cross again. In the meantime, if you should ever happen to read this because I am unable to make my request in person, I hope you do or have forgiven me for deceiving you, not being forthcoming with my attraction to you sooner, and if you felt any anger or confusion for my declaration and reaffirmation of my love for you.

4/2

Hello my Love,

I can't express enough to you how grateful I am to be here, finally seated in 'our' booth on a Saturday evening without having to call ahead to reserve it, and writing to you. Although my shift went by quickly, I still feel exhausted from everything I had to do during it.

    I was greeted by the assistant-department manager who was in the process of "breaking down the truck." I could immediately tell something was bothering him, and when I inquired he told me he had been chewed out earlier that morning for 45 minutes. I surmised it was related to the discussion I had with the store manager yesterday concerning what the department manager had said to me about my helping a customer. I didn't like she was telling me what I was supposed to do to assist the customer which wasn't what the customer had initially requested. You know how I am: I do whatever I'm able to help a customer, even if it takes a little more of my time and is an additional expense to the store. However, she didn't agree with my having to use additional supplies (which

I did even when she scolded me) and even expressing afterward to her why I had done it to the point of almost arguing with her. I wasn't going to allow her to limit what I could do to help, even if it did increase her bonus and improved her performance review. I didn't care especially after this week because of it feeling as though the company underestimates me, doesn't realize of what I am capable, and is making stupid decisions everyday which cause me to have to do more work and expect it to be done on top of all the other tasks they've already given to us.

I'm sorry, 'J', I didn't mean to go off like that. When I was younger, my father would return home from work, sit at the table while the four of us would eat dinner, and talk to my mother about his day at "the plant." Typically, everything he mentioned was negative: a machine breaking down, having to fire an employee, a boss upset about something beyond my father's control, or a situation regarding tension between some of his subordinates. If my father became angry while he was relating the "stressors" of his job, my mother would become upset and they would argue across the table at one another while my sister and I watched from either side as their voices increased in volume and their eating ceased. If their argument reached a certain point of intensity, my mother would rise from her chair, storm off to their bedroom, and slam the door. My father would then call out to her, walk to the closed bedroom door, and continue to yell at her from outside of it. My sister and I, still in our chairs with our plates in front of us, would look at one another, not knowing what to do, and feel somehow guilty for the disagreement we felt as though we may have caused. I can still picture my sister sitting there, saddened by what she had to witness, her eyes beginning to well up, lips turning downward into a frown, and then she would cry. I would try to console her by telling her she hadn't been the cause of their argument and we shouldn't waste our food or they would then direct their anger at us. Eventually, having learned what occurred almost every time he discussed his workday at the dinner table, he avoided the topic altogether, refusing to say anything related to it. The memories of those meals are vivid in my mind in which I'm able to see the expressions on my parents' faces, feel the slamming of the bedroom door shaking the house, and hear my father tell me while he's standing at the door, "Do yourself a favor and don't get married," while the index finger on his right hand appears to be forcefully pushing buttons which weren't there.

My Love, I don't want to repeat the same act of discussing the negative parts of my workday in order to make myself feel better or to cause anyone to be miserable. The last thing I'd ever want to do is to cause you to be unhappy in order to release myself from my own frustrations or "pull you into them" so I won't have to feel as though I'm having to deal with them alone. I suppose that's another reason why I write: to spare anyone from the possibility of being harmed by anything with which I disagree or bothers me. At least on these pages, those stressors can be "quarantined" from my mind and unable to hurt anyone to whom I speak. I realize it may seem selfish to not share these occurrences with you personally, but it's only to spare you from having to suffer from what may be the fault of people who shouldn't have any effect on my personal relationships.

So allow me to tell you about my workday: it was okay. I was able to reassure my supervisor what he had been told by his supervisor regarding something I had said was incorrect. I had the chance to catch up with a former coworker at a previous employer about her recent termination which I felt, from what she told me, was handled improperly and unprofessionally. I impressed the co-managers with my skills in sales by selling a lot of the expensive product we had on special today. For an hour and a half, I had to run the department alone but was assisted in its operation by the new co-manager. He commented, "I don't see how you [the members of the department] keep up with all of this," which I hope caused him to realize how hard we work and how much effort is involved in keeping it presentable. I joked, 'I'd like to see anyone in corporate successfully do what we do especially those who come up with these new additional tasks for us to do,' which caused him to laugh. I also commented, 'I'd like to see our store manager work back here,' which again caused him to be amused. His help was invaluable and I could tell he was impressed by what I was able to do while I was alone. Additionally, I think he was made well aware of the amount of work we have to do and not have the personnel necessary to keep the shelves full and the customers attended to. Because of this observation, I could "hear" a piece of advice my father had told me many times: "Actions speak louder than words." Today, I feel as though someone in management finally knows how it is in our department and we aren't exaggerating. I am content with it. I am also proud of the work I did and anticipate the report on our sales, hoping it was a good day and will justify my not completing some of my assigned tasks. It was busy – that's why.

Well, I have to go meet up with my father in a few minutes. Maybe he will be in a good mood.

Thanks again for listening, 'J'. I still miss you with all of my heart. I hope we will see each other again soon.

Goodnight, my Love.

Hello my Love,

4/6

I assumed I would be here in a happier mood, coming here to have dessert following dinner with my father. Unfortunately, due to the responsibilities of his job, he ended up having to work late. My sister warned me about this occurring when she called me this morning but I dismissed it because I know he would do everything within his ability to uphold his commitment. My sister, predicting accurately what would end up coming true, invited me to dinner with her and her children at another local restaurant which allows my niece to eat for free (my nephew is still too young for solid foods). She was informed earlier her hives are actually a rash from exposure to poison ivy which I can only conclude is making her uncomfortable. Realizing this and the restaurant we were wanting to dine at would be closing in an hour, I suggested we postpone tonight's meal and try it again later. She was content with that, almost sounding relieved because of the errands she said she had to run before our rendezvous. So each of the two people I was hoping to eat with tonight were unavailable. I am sitting here, I believe in the exact booth or near it where we sat during your previous visit. And just like breakfast at another restaurant this morning, I'm here alone, writing, and of course thinking of you.

To further add to my disappointment, I was placed in the same room with a group of locals whom I've seen here almost every Wednesday. It's typically about six to eight of these people ranging in age between 35 to 70 years. They don't appear of low class and are wearing the clothing I've affiliated with this area: boots, denim pants, plaid shirt or one from a clothing line related to golf, and a baseball cap. This I can ignore since they are seated behind me, but what is bothering me right now is the volume of their voices. Thankfully, I had a pair of earplugs in my pocket which have somewhat decreased their noise but are still audible through the pieces of foam in my ear canal. I probably appear ridiculous to them with pieces of purple sticking out of my head, but it's the only way I can concentrate on doing this rather than concerning myself with eating my meal. I can hear myself chewing each bite, wishing now I had ordered an entree "lower in volume," such as a soft taco. But I did order my usual because, especially while sitting in this booth, it reminds me of you.

I'm sorry if I'm making you feel bad. I'm thinking about having to return to the store tomorrow and already know how my shift will begin:

Me: 'Hey, how are you doing?'

Department Manager: "Fabulous" (she says sadly and sarcastically).

Me: 'Sorry to hear that' (sounding sympathetic to her but not to myself).

Department Manager: "Hey, I was wondering why you didn't block the department on Monday night" (which was three days ago. As to why she wants to know about something occurring this many days ago is trivial to me because there is nothing which can be done about it now. She got her freezer organized, cooler floors cleaned, and I left on time – all per her requests. I was only able to take a 10-minute break during my entire eight-and-a-half-hour shift, unable to take a lunch due to no one being available to watch the department and the store manager's desire to have a "good mystery shop" since we are anticipating one because of it usually happening at the beginning of the month. I had no additional help for the last seven hours of my shift EXCEPT another employee from the deli department who took pity on me and wanted to help me because he sees me as a "nice guy." I would like to tell her all of this, but I doubt she would believe me. So I should probably try another method of explaining why it wasn't done).

Me: 'Oh, I must have forgotten.'

'J', I feel as though I cannot free myself from these "weights" preventing me from doing what it is I would want to do. My desires seem so simple: a better job (even if it's within this company) which pays me even a little more, an opportunity to demonstrate of what I am capable, and the chance to go on a date.

That's it.

My "list" used to be longer, but I've had to skim it down to what I regard as attainable. When I wish on the stars at night, at this point what I'm asking for seems reasonable: 'Just something good to happen to make my life better.' The first thing coming to my mind is obvious and impossible given your circumstances. It has been almost five years since I made that wish, five years I've endured without you, five years I've held onto that hope, four years longer than most people would have waited and they themselves would have told me to give up. But I have to have faith, my Love, and trust the Lord is continuing to be involved, not giving up on me, directing me to what it is I must do in order to finally have my wish and intention fulfilled. If loneliness, frustration, anxiety, hopelessness, depression, and patience are what is necessary for me to finally have some happiness, then I'll continue to do His will if it must be done. I know it will be worth it, a small price to pay for a wonderful presence in my life. I just have to continue to survive, remain focused, and endure.

Thank you again for listening, 'J'. Hopefully we will be able to speak to each other again soon. *Todo mi amor contigo.*

A 12 MONTHS WITHOUT YOU   Part 1

4/9

Hello my Love,

I've returned to 'our' restaurant again this evening, seated in the other booth I believe we sat in the day of your previous visit. Coincidentally, it's connected to the one where I was seated the other day. Nonetheless, I somehow "feel" as though you are here, keeping me company, making me almost forget I'm here alone.

As soon as I sat down, I looked around to see the other patrons. To my left, I noticed a man and woman seated on the same side, the gentleman on the outside close to the aisle. The woman on the inside was beautiful...my eyes instantly became fixated on her not because of my attraction to her, but wondering, based on her appearance, if she was you. Looking at your photo affixed to the upper left-hand corner of this notepad, I often wonder if, should you ever appear in my life again, I'll recognize you since it's been over two years since we've seen one another. But I am certain of one thing: you've become prettier during each day we've been apart. What I fear is you won't recognize me. I admit, I've have gained weight over this past year, one of my physicians saying I've increased in weight by 25 pounds. I assumed it was a side effect of my medication but her research concluded a decrease in metabolism was not caused by it. As a result, I have attempted to reduce the amount I consume to the point I don't eat lunch, even while working at the store. I'm hoping, by causing myself to be hungry, my waistline will reduce. Of course I should probably consider what it is I do eat and become more active.

I don't ever recall saying this to you but there is a particular characteristic, one of many, I admire about you, which is you looked beyond my outward appearance and found something you like about me. Perhaps you were aware of its existence for awhile and thought I knew of it, which is why you never mentioned it or I was too afraid to ask. And when I think about it now, I am still concerned as to what you would say and it would be better if I wasn't told. Just having someone have some interest in me, enough to sit across from me during meals and contact me once in awhile made me feel content with the person I was. Sadly, I would like to have this experience again with a woman in the form of a date, but fortune hasn't been with me in this area. Every time I think I may have found "her," she is unavailable and I return to feeling hopeless I will never find a woman with whom I could at least go on a date. I can't tell you how many times I wish I was in yours, my sister's, and my parents' situation: to always have someone there nearby. Your husband, if I haven't said it to you before now, is an extremely lucky man, the luckiest man on this Earth to be the one to take care of you, embrace you, and have you constantly in his life. I couldn't imagine him ever saying he's had a bad workday when he realized he will be able to return home to you at the end of it and you will be there to assure him it will be okay. What I feel toward him I wouldn't regard as jealousy but rather "wishful thinking" I was him or at least possessed a few of the qualities which attracted you enough to marry him. I know what you might say to me if you were seated: "You should pay attention to the qualities you do have." And you're right, which is what I've tried to learn about myself for the past few years, a journey of self exploration and discovery testing my knowledge, limits, skill, experience, emotions, and patience. Patience...that is the one in which has been and is constantly tested to the point I almost want to give up my pursuit toward something, anything better to occur in my life. 'J', I just don't know what to do, uncertain as to whether or not I'm interpreting the Lord's signs correctly. What is His will for me and what does He have planned? Was seeing your mother a few weeks ago a "reminder" I need to continue with what it is I feel I should be doing? Are the people in my life such as Mr. R, Mr. C, and my father present to advise me as to what I'm supposed to do and continue to "hold on" for just a little longer? It's like the train which delayed my arrival here a couple of hours ago. I knew there would eventually be an end to it and I was unable to go anywhere else until it passed. I kept looking toward the back of it, trying to see the last car through the dwindling sunlight, but was missing out on seeing the intriguing graffiti passing in front of me. When will this "train" finally pass, permitting me to continue on my journey to satisfaction and fulfillment? When the gates rise up and the road is unobstructed, will you be there on the other side of the tracks, waiting for me to cross over onto the next phase of my life?

Will you have waited for me too, my Love?

4/13

Hello my Love,

I am grateful for being seated at 'our' booth again, unable to recall the previous time I was here. The restaurant itself is crowded this evening because of their hosting some event for a charity. It's nice to arrive and see something different here rather than the typical and I'll admit, I was hoping to avoid the loud group of locals whom I was seated near last week. The only other concern I have, besides sitting here alone without you, is the distance between the table and the cushion. I'm having to lean forward, my best guess, at a 70 to 75 degree angle which is making me uncomfortable. But it's a small price to pay to feel even somewhat closer to you.

I hope you don't mind, but in order to show Mr. R what I had written during the two consecutive days not scheduled at the store, I provided him with a copy of the letter I had written to you last week. I feel somewhat ashamed for having done it, but if I hope to have my work published someday, I realize I need to "put it out there" and have other people read it. I was somewhat hesitant to give it to him, not only because of the personal feelings I was sharing with you, but especially because it was what I consider an unedited rough draft, unrevised, and written on this medium. The following day, he said he was still reading my "treatise" as he called it, then after two days of not seeing him, that Monday, he was still reading it but had a word to describe it so far: "intense." He also said he's having problems reading it because my handwriting is "making him dizzy" or giving him a headache – I am unable to recall at this moment. From the slant in my words, he concluded I was left-handed, which I've had people assume about me. But I surprised him by saying I'm actually right-handed which I followed by saying a friend of mine in high school said if I ever happen to write a note after having committed a crime, investigators would be looking for someone who writes with their left which would throw off their case. Mr. R also confided some years back, he had seen a fortune teller who was able to "read him perfectly." He then gave me some advice, free of charge, she had given him: "Buy a punching bag." I have since thought about his suggestion and perhaps will do it, not only to release some frustration, but it will lead me to losing weight and becoming fit again. I hope you will forgive me for what I did and if it's of some relief, as it is for me, I didn't share anything from the cards I've written to you. Those words are between you and me and are too personal to be shown to anyone else. What I say to you in those is a secret, thoughts and feelings I've expressed to you and no one else.

It's almost 10 o'clock and there are still people here. I just saw that group of locals leave and noticing how they were looking at me as they walked to the front counter, I assumed they had been made aware of what I said about them last week and would confront me about it. I was prepared to defend what I said, stand by my opinion, and not retract it. A lesson I've learned from my previous in-person interactions with you is I shouldn't be afraid to have a thought and make it known to people. Hiding it isn't dishonest; it's harmful to the person who allows it to affect them negatively. Rather than have it remain in my mind, "eating away" at me, it should be made known to those of whom it is. I suppose this relates to my writing – it shouldn't be tucked away, imprisoned from the world. It should be released, allowed to roam free, interact with others, have an impact on them emotionally. Granted it may not be well received and unwelcomed, but I suppose it's the risk I have to take. I did that here in this booth almost four years ago and I don't regret what I did to this day. Although it may have resulted in my losing a friend, it was better to reveal it rather than continue to have it consume me. I sometimes wonder if you felt I was being selfish, but then you told me you somehow "knew it all along." It just needed to be set free to the world.

Goodnight, *mi amor*.

4/14

Hello my Love,

I realize I'm writing to you two nights consecutively, but after having dinner with my father this evening, I needed some time to reflect on our conversation. We discussed a lot in two hours, some of it sensitive, some personal, some which shouldn't have been overheard by anyone. I decided to come here to 'our' restaurant to have dessert and write about it rather than at the restaurant he and I ate because it would be closing in the next few minutes at nine o'clock. I feel I would be able to focus better on the words in a place such as this rather than the upscale place he and I dined. But mostly, I rather feel as though I'm saying these words to you here. Noticing the direction the conversation was going and the effect it was having on him because of some of the accusations I made, I felt as though it was the perfect moment to make my request to him: to design the cover for my novel I will complete before the end of this year. Before I record his response here, I'm smirking and chuckling because of the irony of it, because of it being the response I would give if someone made such a request to me: "We'll see." The manner, or rather the tone, was one of curiosity, intrigue, and hope, as though I had peaked his interest and gotten his attention. In a way, after I had made him aware of the impact of what he'd said which appeared to upset him, he now needed something to uplift him, rescue him, to free him from the "dungeon" where I had sentenced him. Also, in a similar way, I had "flown in over his city" and "dropped my payload causing damage to his structures." This time, however, I felt it was only right to then help him "rebuild," repair the damage, and provide what other resources he needed. It almost felt as if after the "bombing run" I then dropped off relief supplies or "landed my plane" and assisted in the reconstruction effort. I didn't want to have our conversation, perhaps our final one, to be remembered by him as hurtful. I don't want him to regard me in such a way, even if the words here attempt to dismiss that. At least whenever he reads this, if it happens to be him or you, 'J', he will be made aware I don't claim to be innocent, the recipient of harsh words from him, a victim. I am more at fault than he was while I was trying to "level the playing field" in order to bring him down emotionally to my level, in order to feel like an equal when comparing myself to him. What I didn't realize but what I do now is the man whom I was talking to was more miserable than me with his job, his financial situation, his life. He's at a point which frightens me, selfishly, for my sake but also causes me to feel sympathy for his situation as though there isn't a hint of joy in any of it, with the exception of his grandchildren. It was what I had fantasized about bestowing onto him, anticipating the look of happiness on his face, as he held his first grandson, affirming his name would live for another generation. He would no longer have to be concerned about our "line" ending, an experience which his father likely had when I was held by him initially. Accepting it isn't possible for me at this time and perhaps never, I can at least give him something else: the chance for him to be near to fulfilling one of his dreams, to come close to doing what it is he had considered, to be the person, even if it's brief, he almost became but sacrificed in order to do what he felt would be financially secure if he hoped to be married and start a family of his own. He knew he wouldn't be able to work as an artist and provide them with necessities because of the unsteady income affiliated with being a person who draws or sketches either commercially or professionally. And being the man he is, he wouldn't feel right putting his occupational desires and ambitions before those of his family. I know "the artist" is still within him, appearing to me on only a few rare occasions throughout my life, the man who was at peace and contentment only when he was doodling in the margins of a random document, working on one of his model kits, or including a signature of creativity onto one of the projects he did around his house. This is the man who should be seen by the world, the man who takes pleasure in his effort, the man who is at his greatest. This is the gift I would like to give to him he should have received a long time ago but was unable to accept because of his humility, selflessness, morals, and of course his character: to demonstrate of what he is truly capable to everyone, especially those who criticized, doubted, underestimated, and were given an unfair advantage over him. He needs his "victory," more so than me to restore his faith and remind him of whom he truly is: a passionate, creative, caring, and humble man. This is the person with whom I would like to be acquainted and meet the person whom I'm destined to become.

'J', if something incapacitates me and causes me to be unable to say this to him, please give him these words so he will know this is how I truly felt toward him. Although this letter was meant for you, I wanted to share my thoughts about someone to whom I aspire and want to make proud of me. In a way, the relationship you seem to have with your father inspired me to have one similar with mine. Thank you for doing this – narrowing the gap having formed between us. Thank you for helping to bring a father and son closer together this evening and once again for listening to me, my Love.

A 12 MONTHS WITHOUT YOU   Part 1

4/16
Hello my Love,

I'm sorry for writing to you again so soon. Because of the day I've had, I was looking forward to writing to you, hoping in some way you can hear me and make me feel better. So in case I forget to say it, I appreciate you for being here to listen.

What should have been a happy family occasion for me turned out to be a reminder of my relationship status. Being the only person at the baptism of my nephew who wasn't involved with someone caused me to feel lonely and depressed. Everyone there, even the deacon presiding over it had some one special in their lives, someone whom they could refer to as "dear," someone who would take care of them if something devastating occurred to them, someone to say, "I love you," to them at some point during the day. I woke up this morning alone, managed to get through the day alone, and will go to sleep alone. I had your photo, the same one at the top-left-hand corner of this page, in my shirt pocket in order to feel as though at least one person in the world at one time cared for me.

I'm somewhat ashamed I feel this way but I am happy both sides of my sister's family were able to share this moment together. My sister did have some concern about her sister-in-law attending the ceremony but it didn't appear to have affected her mood. Sadly the only other people who were there were another married couple and their daughter who are friends of my sibling. The deacon looked curious, wondering if anyone else would be showing up, but 13 plus I ended up gathered in the Church at 11 to 12 o'clock. I was kind of hoping more people would be there, perhaps the pastor changing his mind or fitting it into his schedule. I suppose a smaller group was better and the privacy of it allowed for us to not have to feel as though we were vying for the parishioners' attention. I'm sorry, 'J', I'm just still bothered at what a waitress, who regards me as being her friend, said last night and used certain words to describe me. She doesn't know what it's like to be rejected again, and again, and again and the impact of it bringing you to a point in which you want to give up, death appearing to be the only way to escape the endless cycle, the allure of it beckoning to you, calling you, the easiness of it always present, its open arms awaiting to embrace you and take you away from the harshness and disappointments of life. Those who were involved and present toward the end of my existence would finally know the pain, the heartache, and the sadness causing me to do what I felt would give me peace.

If it means that I'm supposed to be with the person that I'm meant to be with, I don't mind the wait. I'll be patient. But nothing's definite. If you find someone who makes you better, don't let them go. It sounds as though she keeps you going.
                                                          -A busboy at this restaurant

Thank you for listening again, my Love, and for keeping me going. Goodnight from *A12*.

4/20

Hello my Love,

I had no idea where else I would be eating dinner this evening, however my sister called me earlier and said she wanted to eat at a local Italian restaurant. The fact I had a coupon for our meal was convincing to her, so I met up with her, her husband, and their kids. Aside from my niece misbehaving at the beginning of it, the experience was pleasant. I can't believe how much my nephew continues to grow in between the times I see him, the increasing amount of hair appearing on his head, and the more expressive he becomes. Sometimes I feel as though I'm holding my infant self, wondering if my father has the same thoughts as he's holding his grandson.

My workday was unusual because of it not only being on a day I'm normally not scheduled and lasting only four hours, but my department manager was surprisingly in a good mood. She informed me she usually has to do the "change over" by herself and there is a lot for her to do, especially coming off of this particular sale. I arrived cautious, assuming she had been told about the negative comments I had made about her regarding my schedule this past Sunday. I was anticipating her questioning me as to why I said what I did and the reason I didn't speak with her about my concerns directly. Thankfully, she didn't act upset or she was hiding it surprisingly well. I decided to go along with her mood, doing whatever I was able to be helpful and cooperative, and even remained after the end of my shift to discuss company-related topics such as upper management's unawareness of what actually occurs at a store, are all provided with the same model of car, and expect more work out of us but without providing us additional labor hours. We concluded they don't have their heads stuck up their a--es, but instead each others as though they are better than everyone else within the firm. In addition to these topics, she and I speculated as to the fate of our location and assume it will be announced during the meetings tomorrow it will be closed once the new location opens. I already know if it occurs, many of my customers won't shop at the new one. Given my epiphany yesterday evening, I don't care what happens not only because I don't have a say in the decision, but even if I protest and attempt to convince them otherwise the act will be pointless. She and I realized although we are part of an advertised "family" no one higher up in the firm wants to listen to those who work at the locations. As I've been writing this, I've been thinking about what I'd like to say to them at the meeting, envisioning the words flowing from my mouth, countering every argument they make, standing up to them for what they've done to mess up the company, and accuse them of ignoring those whom they should actually be asking for suggestions: us. Of course, we aren't sure as to what they'll say tomorrow, so it's probably better I focus my attention on the completion of my novel. I have to remind myself again my path isn't with this company and hopefully I will not be with them for much longer. I can see where they are headed and this new location will be another "nail in their coffin," another "breach in their hull," another "hole in their tire." I'd rather not be buried with them, sink with them, or be stranded with them. It's time for me to pursue something better.

Well, the restaurant is about to close so I better get going. Thank you again for listening, 'J', and I'm sorry it was mostly about work. Booth *A11* kept me company this evening, as though you were here. Hopefully we will be eating here sometime soon. Goodnight, my Love.

A12 MONTHS WITHOUT YOU   Part 1

4/21

Hello my Love,

I apologize for writing to you again so soon. After what I did today, the only person whom I feel I could adequately express what occurred is to you.

I hadn't planned on dining here again, but I couldn't see myself recording these thoughts while seated at my desk, eating a previously-frozen pizza, and distracted by my urge to go on the computer and see what happened while I was at the store meeting held earlier.

It was at the meeting the DM (district manager) announced to about 10 to 15 other employees along with the HR (human resources) representative for our district, the store manager, and his co-manager trainee gathered in the warm and abysmal stock room our location would be closing in about a year. It was intimidating, the DM standing directly across from me, his compatriots with their long-sleeved shirts, opened collars, and company logo stitched on the left-hand side above the pocket with their name tags on the opposite side. Meanwhile, I'm standing in my white-long-sleeved shirt, black necktie having just been redone with a Windsor knot, sleeves rolled up to my elbows, holding my black notebook in front of my left hand while my right is tucked behind me. My feet were about a foot and a half to about two feet apart, as if I were standing at "parade rest" formation when I was in JROTC (Junior Reserve Officer Training Corp). But I wasn't resting – I was waiting for the right moment to "strike" while appearing as though I was oblivious to what was being said by a man whom I had reported to HR (coincidentally the same man standing one person away, the store manager, away from him) about two months ago and assumed because of my accusation of nepotism and an investigation uncovering additional infractions, he and his son would no longer be employed with the company and thus allowing all employees to have a fair chance of advancing within the firm based on merit and hard work rather than because of their familial relationship to someone in a position to plan their career path.

I admit, I was hesitant to say anything, wondering if the HR rep had decided to disclose what I had suspected about this man. But I didn't allow that or the fear of any repercussions of what I would say affect my words. Once he (the DM) had confirmed what it was my coworkers and I had suspected earlier in the week, I felt it was time to "take a risk" as my grandfather had advised, and speak on behalf of not only what I felt in my heart, but most importantly my customers whom I regard as acquaintances and some of them as close friends.

I began with asking for permission to speak candidly, and once given, appearing reluctant by the DM, I stepped into the center of the circle, your photo in my shirt pocket, appearing as though you were watching me, cheering me on, encouraging me as I delivered my words without having rehearsed them and making up the speech as I spoke. To boost my confidence, I even pretended you were one of the people whom I was addressing while turning to each of my coworkers in order to make them feel included in what I was saying, perhaps even gain their support. I went so far as to revert to another time when I knew I had to take another risk, "putting it all on the line" because I may never have another chance to do so: when I first declared my love to you, while holding your hand, coincidentally in the booth behind me at this restaurant where I am dining at this moment. And similar to that speech almost four years ago, I cannot recall most of what I said, a lot of it forgotten because I was so focused on delivering my message instead of hoping to recall it later. But I felt as though I had "said my peace" on both occasions and have no regrets about anything I conveyed. What's important to me is I was not afraid of the impact it would have nor had any expectations of the effects. No one applauded or followed up afterward with their own words of support; it wasn't that type of crowd. I am somewhat disappointed none of them would speak up in agreement with me and I can't fault them for it. They have to consider what they value and for right now their job is their livelihood. I couldn't ask them to jeopardize it in order for me to prove a point and no decent leader would make such a request from anyone. So for now, I assume the only result of what I said will be my termination as soon as I begin my shift tomorrow. I will do my best to prepare for this eventuality by creating a new resignation letter rather than provide them with the pleasure of seeing the look of disappointment on my face as they give me the news. This will be the second time I've quit this company and hopefully the final time I do so. But it's okay – I've been wanting to leave them for awhile because of their limiting my potential by not offering me a position utilizing my education and experience. I was sincerely hoping they were different from 'our' previous employer and really, they are all the same. I kind of feel sorry for them; they would have both benefited greatly.

They both had their chance.

Goodnight, my Love, and again, my immense gratitude for listening.

PAUL S. DOIZÉ

4/23

Hello my Love,

I'm sorry if I sound exhausted and my handwriting is illegible, but I'm tired. I was told to begin my shift two hours and 15 minutes after I was initially scheduled. Upon my arrival, I noticed our "prep area" was a disaster. My other coworker was working on the new shipment of lunch meat and was about to finish. Thankfully, the grinder hadn't been used nor any of the other pieces of equipment. I focused my tasks on restocking the "fresh-meat" shelves, especially the steaks we had on sale. Before his shift ended, I asked my coworker to "block" the lunch meat because I didn't want to have to be overwhelmed with doing it later. About a minute before he had to leave or else go over, the power in the entire store went out and our back-up generators came on although most of the lights were either off or flickering, creating a somewhat "club" atmosphere. The co-manager trainee asked me to begin to ask our customers to exit the store for safety reasons, unfortunately having to do so directly to them since our intercom system was unavailable. After asking one woman who said, "The hell I'm leaving," I gave up and instead went up front to bag groceries in order to, really, just get them out of the store so none of them would be hurt. I was then told to make sure none of the customers who remained were permitted to go into the produce, deli, and my section since they were almost dark. Once all of the customers left, we closed the store and assessed what needed to be done to save our product.

The young women from up front, at the direction of the co-manager trainee, began to take long pieces of plastic sheeting and tape them over the dairy cases while another group of employees removed the beef, pork, and chicken from my department's shelves, the same ones I had been trying to fill since my arrival. Each employee took a section, placed the product in a cart, and we lined it up in the stock room in order to put it in the meat cooler at one time. My department manager soon arrived, appearing concerned about the product being taken off of the shelves and thrown into grocery carts without any consideration for possibly damaging the items, saying she hopes she "would receive credit." At the moment we were about to put a long piece of plastic over the entire lunch meat case, the power came back on and we were told to wait 20 minutes before putting anything back on the shelf. We were also informed we would be reopening the store in an hour but it turned out to be about in about 10 to 15 minutes rather than the 60. I spent the remainder of my shift with two of my coworkers refilling the shelves the women from up front had just cleaned, under the assumption we would have the next hour to prepare. I was then able to begin my cleaning, putting away my cases, washing my dishes, and straightening up the department. The co-manager trainee approved of the appearance and was okay with me receiving 45 minutes of overtime since, because of the outage, we had to condition the department. For the record, I am thankful to everyone who helped, stepped up during the emergency, and cooperated with each other with the co-manager overseeing it. Since they're about to close, I'm going to go ahead and call it a night. Thank you for listening, my Love, while I write to you from booth *A12*, 'our' booth, *mi amor*.

A 12 MONTHS WITHOUT YOU   Part 1

4/27

Hello my Love,

I have been blessed with being able to sit in 'our' booth this evening. I was afraid my tardiness would cause me to be seated somewhere else, but considering this group who was here last week and again tonight (one man in particular) I'm glad I have my earplugs with me. If I didn't have them I would stuff pieces of wet paper towels in my ears or else I might find myself standing up, walking over to where he is, and punching him right in the face, coincidentally or ironically, maybe both or neither, with the hand with which I'm writing.

Now that both plugs are in, I can feel as though I can concentrate, as if no one else is here, I cannot be bothered. I realize it may seem mean or even hypocritical to say, especially since I'm writing a letter to someone whom I wish, with all my heart, was here with me instead of sounding as though I would rather be alone. There is a Hispanic couple at my 10 o'clock, about middle-aged, eating in almost silence or with few words (I can see their lips moving) exchanged between them. Their presence, as unusual as it may sound, is reassuring to me this is indeed a good restaurant and allows me to pretend I'm in another country far away from this town.

I was unable to write for the past two days because of a relapse I had with a disease from which I had a couple of months ago. I initially assumed it was allergies or sinuses because of this time of year, but given the weakness I've experienced along with the intense heat I felt causing me to perspire even while taking a shower, I was convinced I had another cold or something related to the flu shot I received about six months ago. Whatever it is, it caused me to lose two valuable days of writing but has also reaffirmed my resolve to complete a novel before the end of the year, as I promised myself I would.

While I was donating blood today, the woman attending to me had an interesting tattoo on the bottom of her left arm: it was of two characters from a stop-motion-animation film which came out when I was in the eighth grade. The two film protagonists were holding each other in their arms, as if she was leaning onto him for support. The only color of ink used in the design aside from black was a single red strand strand connecting the two characters at their hearts. When I asked the attendant the meaning of it she said, "He's using his thread to mend her heart," which I concluded was the reason he was holding her. The attendant admitted the image wasn't finished, but given the message it was attempting to convey, I personally thought it looked great as it is. If only it were that simple to fix another person's heart, especially someone you love...to have a "strand" originating from one person and using it to suture or at least "fill in" the part which is injured or empty. A single line connecting two individuals, using the strength and vitality one has to heal and sustain the other; a piece of them becomes a piece of the other, and not just a random piece but the most important, one to make them whole again. I can't imagine the pain a person would feel, living everyday knowing they are incomplete, searching for whatever could "fit" in the space. Their existence is meaningless without what it is which will give them happiness, contentment, peace. The only reason they keep going is the one thing temporarily filling their emptiness: hope. It "drives" them, sustains them enough to continue, powers them through their journey but isn't meant to replace what it is they require, to make life better for them, to allow them to experience what it is to feel as though they are cherished, thought about, and of course loved. As difficult as the journey was, the hardships endured, the endless waiting, and the disappointments since forgotten, it was all worth it for what connected her to him, bringing them together at last.

Well, that group just left and the restaurant is about to close. I should let the staff finish up so they can call it a night. Thank you again for listening, 'J', and I hope even with this sickness, I was able to make sense. Goodnight, my Love.

5/4

Hello my Love,

This is the first chance I've had to write anything today. Two consecutive days off from work and I had to return today. About five to ten minutes after my arrival we were informed the health department had arrived causing us to scramble to make the area look better than it already was. My department manager had to leave during the inspection to begin her vacation so I was alone during the remainder of it except for the co-manager checking in periodically on their status. Fortunately, our scores for both of our departments ended up being higher (a 98% for meat and 96.5% for seafood) than one of our "flagship" stores, one which is overseen by a son of the DM. Sadly, this is likely the last time our department will be inspected because of it closing in about a year. I'm just content we did well and it shows the company our "piece-of-s--t" store, as I'm sure they regard us, actually does well compared to the ones they've renovated.

I wasn't able to again take "lunch" because of no one able to cover my department so I spent a few minutes in my usual spot, having a snack and a drink while keeping an eye on the department. I'm still hoping Mrs. S will be able to do something to put in a good word for me where she works so I can be at a place allowing me to take my lunch during all of my shifts and will compensate me better. I really need my job situation to improve, 'J'; I'm not sure how much more I can endure from this place, especially how they underestimate me. I feel they look down up me, regard me as idiotic, and assume I'm incapable of more. The store manager...I revile him, almost to the point where I want to tell him off and then spit on him. He disgusts me, angers me, causes me to want to punch him in the face and then say, 'So they think you're some golden boy, huh? I'm the one they should have placed in your position.' Meanwhile, he's being made to look like some type of "hero" because of the efforts of my coworkers and I with barely the personnel required to operate. We've lost several of them since his arrival, mostly because they don't like his style of managing by intimidation, overworking people, and not showing any appreciation or recognition. He's a bad manager who doesn't deserve his position, especially with his recent action of having our co-manager demoted by telling HR he was performing poorly. That alone causes me to despise and distrust him, hoping his superiors will see him for the person he is.

But they won't do anything. He's a member of their "club" and the club itself will remain in place within the firm. I tried what I could without putting my job at risk. I don't consider it a failure but an "impossible victory." No matter what I could do to make the correct personnel in the company aware of what is unfairly occurring, there's no point because nothing will be done to correct it. I realize I'm outmatched and overwhelmed. So I have to pray some other job in hopefully a different sector will become available. I'm tired of retail and I'm certain it's tired of me. I'm a "relic" of a different time, recalling what the manager said during one of our meetings: "Efficiency was the name of the game five years ago. Now it's all about 'the new system' and that's not going away anytime soon."

I need to refocus my thoughts on my novel, think about it continuously, pursue it with all my heart, remain attentive, and remind myself the sooner I complete it, the sooner I may be released from this "prison," doing what it is I'm meant to do and forever leave that manager and his "group" behind, the ones who are holding me back and regarding themselves as superior to everyone, especially my coworkers.

Thank you again for listening, my Love, and I'm sorry for burdening you with my problems. I appreciate someone hearing them so I don't have to retain them in my mind.

5/7

Hello my Love,

I speak to you once again, thankfully from 'our' booth this evening. Upon my arrival at this restaurant, I noticed there were cups and a basket on the table. Realizing the previous occupants had left, I requested it, even if it meant having to wait a few minutes for it to be cleaned. I assured the staff they could take their time; I was willing to be patient for the place I wanted to sit during my meal. Because I skipped eating lunch instead preferring to read and have a snack during it, I decided to "treat" myself to an entree rather than my typical appetizer/meal. I ended the work week with 39.25 hours, part of the overage because of being asked by the co-manager trainee to remain later and produce some backup product for the remainder of the evening. My coworker wasn't happy when I informed him of what I was told to do, causing him to throw the hose on the floor he was using to clean the cutting boards. I realize he was frustrated and upset. I was delaying his closing duties but I assured him I was only doing what I was told. Whether that was of any comfort to him I'm uncertain, but minutes later I heard him joking and laughing with a customer so I assume his outburst was simply a way of relieving the stress having built up as a result of how busy our department was today. Working with him on and off for the past four years, it was uncharacteristic of him to react in such a way, especially for a man of his age and what he's probably experienced throughout his time spent in retail. I can't imagine how much he has had to endure, the people with whom he has had to tolerate, and the countless useless tasks he has been told to complete. I feel sorry for him and I also respect this man for what he has done in order to survive.

'J', I look around this restaurant at the people seated with their spouses, children, or friends. I sit here alone again, wishing you or someone else was seated across from me, telling me about their day, a pleasant experience they had, informing me of their educated opinion about a current event or decision they made. Several times throughout this week, I found myself on the verge of crying, wondering what it is causing me to be constantly alone, no one (a person, anyway) awaiting for me to return to them at the house, a missed call or text message from someone wanting me to contact them. What is it, my Love, that has made me become this way, be devoid of anyone having the desire to be with me, in my presence, enjoying my company? Am I really so horrible of a person, having an attitude or "air" about me making people not to want to be around me? Am I so unlike the residents of this area they regard me as an outcast or pariah?

As I told my direct supervisor earlier, 'I just have bad luck.' That's the only reason I can think of for my current status, unless God is "pissed off" at me for something I've done wrong, the list being long and the items countless. I would hate to think the sins I've committed are being held against me, the punishment being solitude in order to think about what it is I've done wrong and the consequences of those infractions.

It feels like when I was a child who was sent to my room because of a possession of my parents I broke, a curse word they overhead from me, or having fought with my sister. I wait in my room, sit on the bed, ponder the effect of what I had done, and wait to be released/paroled from my confinement. That's the worst part...the ignorance of not knowing when one or both of them will enter the room and pardon me from my "cell," returning to the world a freed and rehabilitated person. When will I be freed from this loneliness, 'J'? When will I be told I can return to the world populated with my friends and someone who is eagerly awaiting my arrival? When will I be informed I have served my sentence and my lesson has been learned? When will I have someone special in my life?

Goodnight, my Love, and thanks for listening.

PAUL S. DOIZÉ

5/11

Hello my Love,

I just got off of work about 20 minutes ago. Surprisingly, it was early for me since I'm used to staying there until I absolutely have to leave before I go into the next 15-minute increment. There were other tasks I could have done in those minutes, but I didn't want to take time away from what is important to me and this evening it was to write to you here in a booth connected to the one we sat in that day because *A12* was occupied. The group of Christians who were absent last Wednesday is here this evening seated at a long table toward the front of the restaurant. I'm glad I remembered to put my earplugs in my pants pocket or else I'd have to listen to a particular member of their group whose voice, for some reason, bothers me. Their children are being distracted by a movie playing on a cell phone, coincidentally one my niece apparently likes and I have yet to watch. Given the attention it has received and the frequency of "clips" I've caught of it, I wouldn't doubt I've seen it in its entirety by now. To my left at the other row of booths is another diner sitting alone, a local, given his attire of a baseball cap, short-sleeved t-shirt, and boots of a cowboy rather than a construction worker or someone who works in an area requiring such footwear. He is looking at his phone, sometimes with one hand or both, appearing as though he is transfixed by what is in front of him. The light from the screen illuminates his face and if my vision was better I could probably read the text on his forehead, cheeks, and chin although the words would be backwards. But I don't have any interest in his conversation; I'd rather be speaking to you.

Our store manager began his vacation to the relief of my coworkers and me. My department manager returned from hers today, her face tanned from the beach yet she still had the same sullen expression she always has while working. While she was away, she interviewed for a similar position at another location. She said they have to talk to another candidate but hopes she will be offered the job and then she and her husband can move there. And then I won't have to endure her sour disposition, lack of attention and enthusiasm for what we accomplish, and scolding and condemning my coworkers and me for what wasn't done under the assumption it was due to our laziness. I'm certain the store manager would like to see her depart as well, given the aggressiveness she has shown toward him. His refraining from speaking to her, she feels, is a "win" for her so she doesn't have to interact with him. It seems as though it's not out of fear or intimidation he avoids her – it's so he possibly won't have a confrontation with her. She should be ashamed of having a boss who could help her but won't because she may start a fight with him. My direct supervisor has even mentioned he may be leaving soon to return to his previous employer but would consider remaining if they (management) offered him her position. Then again, could you imagine if they offered it to me rather than him? More than likely, the store manager will use this as a chance to put one of his own "people" in place, someone just like him, loyal to him, whom he can control. At that point, it will definitely be time for me to leave, more so than it was today and every shift before it. I sincerely wish the Lord has a plan for me to be disassociated with this place soon on my own terms rather than termination. Hopefully I will be made aware of an available position in another job sector, one not having to be overseen by people well connected amongst themselves, only looking out for one another, not allowing anyone to ascend within the company unless they're a "member" of their group.

The staff is doing their cleaning and I should probably leave to let them finish shutting down. Thanks again for listening, my Love. May my life, as well as my luck, improve soon.

A 12 MONTHS WITHOUT YOU Part 1

5/14

Hello my Love,

I write to you from, luckily, 'our' booth but in the midst of a noisy restaurant. Upon my approach, I noticed the parking lot was full which meant most of the diners would probably be eating on the outdoor patio because of the beautiful evening. From what I learned last night, this is also the prom for at least one high school's students who may have chosen this place for their meal before attending the event. Also I learned before they enter the main area where their prom is taking place, the students will have to take a breathalyzer test in order to prohibit anyone who has been drinking. I'm surprised the adolescents would have to be subjected to that, but I suppose a lot has changed in the years since I've been out of high school, especially with the invention of social media and the increase in violence at those institutions. Then again, a mass shooting occurred at another school during the final months of my senior year. Since then, there have been more and I'm sure others not receiving any news coverage.

Originally I wasn't scheduled to work today, but the co-manager trainee asked me a few days ago if I would be interested in doing so. Being in retail this long, I've become accustomed to working on Saturday's. I realize there are many people who have jobs in which they "live for the weekend," looking forward to having two consecutive days off and then returning the following Monday. Once in awhile, I will be scheduled to have two weekdays off in a row and then be scheduled to work on the third. During the second day, I begin to become comfortable with this and then start to dread the next shift. I couldn't imagine feeling this way week after week, year after year, until I find a more enjoyable profession or it's time for me to retire. I guess that's one of the hidden benefits of my job: having a day off when others don't. Also it can be frustrating to realize, although I'm away from the store that day, I'm unable to forget I have to return to it in a matter of hours; it's as if I'm always there with short spans of freedom in between shifts.

The group of people at the long table next to me has left and the restaurant has become quieter. I looked over and found a cellphone underneath one of the chairs. I'm certain at some point in the evening someone will panic, wonder where it is, and what happened to it. Giving it to a waiter, he went to the lobby where members of the group were paying for their meals. I assume one of them claimed it and will be spared from fear later this evening, coincidentally something I would frequently wish for before I was prescribed my medication last year. Anytime I can "rescue" anyone from the intense worry is my way of repaying a debt I feel I owe the Lord for calming my mind.

In the half an hour before the restaurant closes, several more small groups have arrived. One member of one of those groups is a young woman who is wearing a t-shirt bearing the logo of my alma mater. It reminds me of the dreams I've been experiencing, the ones disturbing me, causing me to ponder the message behind their frequency. I've also been thinking a lot about what you said during your previous in-person visit: "You don't see the world like everyone else," which I still regard as a sincere compliment especially originating from you. Your statement, the dreams, what I continue to discover about myself...all of these cause me to consider my role within the world, what it is I'm meant to do, what I'm suppose to accomplish, whom I'm to become someday. If the dreams are of any indication perhaps my path involves my returning to the university or some other facility of higher education. Maybe the observations made by you, Mr. R, and others not of familial relation are meant to "direct" me in a set direction, maintain it, and not deviate or become distracted or delayed until I reach that destination, when and wherever it is. What if this moment, along with the many, many others before this one and the others afterward are meant to occur in order to provide me the opportunity to "figure things out," reflect on what I've experienced and endured these past five years, to "shape" me into the person who awaits me, and when the moment arrives, I am the person whom they have been eagerly and patiently anticipating? I admit, 'J', it's difficult, almost impossible to maintain this mindset. But, as I experienced yesterday, I have to believe the Lord is watching over me, guiding me, and involved in my life continuously. When I have <u>doubt</u>, He works through people to restore my <u>faith</u>. When I am in <u>despair</u>, He sends me "signs" of <u>hope</u> to keep going. When I experience <u>darkness</u> in my heart, He <u>lights</u> it with brief spans of happiness which counteract the bad luck with which I feel as though I am cursed. And when I'm <u>sad</u>, at the point of giving up and walking away from what it is causing me to be stressed and overwhelmed with my burdens, He reminds me of the <u>joys</u> in my life such as the youthful vigor of my niece, the kind smile and laugh of my nephew, and the unknown expression of bliss on my parents' faces whenever they are with their grandchildren. Someday I hope God will forgive me for the feelings of <u>hatred</u> I've had and currently possess toward some people while also realizing <u>love</u> is and has always been present, even in those moments of physical lust. For the <u>injuries</u> particularly those of an emotional form I've done to those whom have negatively affected me, I ask to be <u>pardoned</u> from those, realizing I am a person of many faults – envy, jealousy, and resentment being the worst. But above all, I hope the Lord has some understanding sympathy toward what it is I feel for a certain woman whom I still love even though she is married. I cannot deny what it is in my heart, ignore the passion I feel for her, it is her to whom I am writing this evening, a woman whom I sincerely wish was with me here at this moment, listening to these words as I speak them to her across this table, looking into her beautiful eyes on her freckled face, while holding her soft gentle hand in mine.

Perhaps, the Lord willng, I will experience it again. I just have to patiently wait for it if when the moment occurs. And I hope the moment happens soon, when He feels I've waited long enough and the time is right, I'll be ready for it.

Then, I won't feel so alone.

Thank you, my Love, for again listening to me and keeping me company. I hope you're okay and my prayers for you are being heard by Him. May 'our' paths cross again, and when they do, we will be seated here in *A12*. Goodnight and my heart is with you, my Love.

A12 MONTHS WITHOUT YOU   Part 1

5/18

Hello my Love,

I just finished dinner with my former roommate here at 'our' restaurant. The two-hour conversation he and I had focused on improving my occupational situation. Unfortunately I realized this before my arrival, even during the couple of days leading up to it feeling as though I would need to defend my actions and the direction of my life. I appreciate what he's attempting to do, admire his motivation to want to see me employed at a better job, and remind me I'm capable of achieving more than for what I give myself credit.

   I'm not seated in 'our' booth, but rather in the other section near a painting of what I believe is a farmer harvesting agave nectar. To my left are two of the hostesses and then behind them is the manager. To my upper left in a booth seated alone is one of the busboys, a young man who asked me a couple of weeks ago about what it is I write. He is actually one of the few people employed here who has inquired about what it is they see me do. The waitress who attended to my former roommate and me and now only me while I eat dessert is a young woman whom, after about a year living in another state, has returned to this area. As she told me during our brief conversation a few minutes ago, "There is such a thing as Southern hospitality." 'What is unusual,' I conveyed to her, 'is I feel more comfortable talking with her now than I did with my recent dinner companion and also sitting in this area with the other staff members.'

My Love, I'm not sure what it is about me not wanting to come completely forward with what it is I feel in my heart regarding what it is I want to do with my life. I understand from where it is my former roommate comes and what are the priorities in his life: money, a good job, and involvement with women. I can't fault him for those because of his age and previous circumstances. But the fact is, he and I are different ages, separated by about nine years in two different decades. Most people at my place in life are settled with a spouse, children, a home, and a career. He is where he wants to be right now, following the path most travel and is where they should be. I have always felt "left behind," struggling to keep up, having to work harder than everyone else because of "disadvantages" I possess. He and I both acknowledge we didn't originate from families who were "well off" financially nor did we have the luxury of all of our monetary needs paid for during our college attendance. We both have had jobs in which we were underutilized, underappreciated, and undervalued. He, as I've accepted from my company, told me of the "hierarchy" existing among upper management and I won't be able to successfully become involved nor want to be part of it." I suppose he's correct, however it would be much better than what I'm doing there now. Maybe I would be slightly regarded as a person rather than of the same level as a meat/cheese slicer, an electric scale, or the seafood steamer – easily replaceable because of the one or two tasks it was built to do.

I know there is a lot more to who I am besides what is

seen on the surface and on a resume. There's probably much, much more than what you read of these words, but this is as close as I'm able to completely reveal due to my self-regarded complexity, sometimes comparing myself to a diamond because of my possessing many "facets."

He and I both know we aren't entitled to anything because of our educations or from what we've endured occupationally, but it doesn't mean we can't fight for what it is we desire, even if they are easily acquired by most people.

I've been here for about three hours and they are about to close, so I suppose it's time for me to depart.

My apologies to the hostess, for forgetting her name and finally recalling it later during my visit here.

My most sincere gratitude to my waitress for sharing something personal about herself, being a fantastic attendant, and allowing me to remain here in her section until I felt satisfied with what I had written this evening.

And to you, my Love, thank you again for listening, for being a kind face who inspires me, and keeping me company once again.

5/19

Hello again my Love,

I realize I just spoke to you this time yesterday evening, but my shift ended at the store and I didn't feel like returning to the house and having dinner alone. So, as a way of celebrating my repair of my phone, not having anyone to cover the department to take a lunch, and only eating a honey bun today, I thought I would come here and, thankfully, write to you from *A12*. Surprisingly, my "usual" arrived with diced tomatoes on it, and after taking a bite of it, I'm glad I decided to come here after all.

    My Love, something my former roommate said during our conversation here yesterday has been on my mind. He said I should regard my writing as more of a "hobby" and instead focus on finding a better job.

    "A hobby..."

    "...until I find a better job."

    I feel as though he slapped me in the face, belittled it, and regarded it as something I do in my spare time.

    'J', I don't think of this as simply something I do to keep

busy or to "pass the time." In fact, I put in about as much time and effort doing this as I do at my job, thinking about what I would want to write later while doing my assigned mundane tasks (what you're reading a product of today's shift). I prefer to consider this my passion, my identity, my destiny.

I feel as though I was created to do this, everything I've experienced throughout my life influencing me to be who it is I'm meant to be.

I somehow know, with every fiber of my being, I am meant to do "something" important and meaningful in my life. It's as if I have these brief "flashes" of what I eventually do, sometimes speaking in front of a large crowd, such as at a commencement ceremony or meeting, and telling them how I ended up standing there, what has happened to me, conveying meaningful and inspirational words. Maybe I'm receiving an award or honorary degree, but neither of those is important to me – what is of importance is the occurrences and events of my life having resulted in me standing behind a podium, on a stage, saying what it is I had prepared beforehand, while many sets of eyes look at me and the same amount of ears are listening attentively. I don't expect a standing ovation, let alone any applause when I'm finished. I just know I have a message to deliver and it is meant to be heard. That message, whatever it is, isn't meant to be vengeful, demeaning, or cause anyone to become upset. It is a "reflection" of the life I've lived at this point, the lessons I've learned, and what it is resulting in me being the person standing there. I may be meant for greatness or at least to do better than almost everyone assumed.

Almost, because a few people throughout my life have somehow known I could and will do better.

I don't expect to become wealthy because of this or even "set for life." The most I would hope to achieve would be to have enough to be comfortable, to not have to worry about the electricity being cut off because of a delayed payment, to not have to wait until payday in order to mail a check, to have to only consider the appetizers as a main entree. My former roommate and I agreed the most we could hope for from life would be contentment. But I feel as though there could be something better, something more than "barely tolerating what you do for a job." What about those people who are fortunate enough to have a career they love or do what it is that makes them happy and get paid to do it?

I would like to become one of those people and I don't believe I can achieve it by doing this as a "hobby."

I just can't do it because of the effect it may have on me.

It may destroy the best part of me, the most unique, the significant.

I have to continue to listen to "the voice" motivating me to sit here, to record what it is on my mind, to create something of importance, something assuring me whatever I was doing is what I was meant to do all along.

Thank you for listening again, my Love.

5/21

Hello my Love,

I'm astonished to say this, but I didn't think I would be speaking to you from 'our' booth this evening. I had initially arrived here about 40 minutes ago, but when the hostess was about to seat me, for some reason I reached for my back right pocket and realized my wallet was gone. I told her I would be back shortly and returned to the house to find I had left my wallet in my work pants, having forgotten to take it out and put it on the nightstand as I typically do when I go into my bedroom to get cleaned up after my shift. On my second trip to the restaurant, I passed by the store and noticed my co-worker from today (the man you met the day during your last visit) exiting the store while holding an umbrella. Assuming he may want a ride to his home or somewhere else, I turned around at the next street, stopped at the curb, and picked him up. He was going to walk to the "gaming place" about a quarter to a half a mile away up the road and remain there until his wife's shift ends about an hour and a half later. I then returned to the restaurant, was greeted again, and pleasantly surprised they knew which booth I usually requested and additionally, had it reserved with a basket of chips and a bowl of salsa waiting for me. One of the hostesses remarked she didn't think I would return and I didn't feel it necessary to disclose what I had forgotten when I had initially arrived about 20 to 30 minutes ago. When I was seated one of the staff members arrived to welcome me and offered to replace the chips which had probably cooled and been exposed for a little while. After ordering my entree, I wanted to wash my hands and used the restroom near the entrance of the restaurant. On my way back to the table, I noticed a waitress at one of the other restaurants I used to go to before it closed in October of 2014. She was seated with her two children and mother on the cushions in the lobby. Her fiancé arrived a few minutes later and stopped at my table before he was notified to meet his family in the other room.

What is unusual about this evening is all the coincidences occurring because I had initially forgotten my wallet. Had I been seated the first time, my coworker wouldn't have gotten a ride, I may not have encountered the waitress and her fiancé, and I likely wouldn't be sitting here in a booth which somehow makes me feel closer to you, as though I'm reliving that day here almost four years ago.

We may regard our lives as a "mess" of random events happening chaotically, but this evening, at least to me, reminds me there perhaps might be a plan in place, connecting everything and everyone in a "web," making sure moments take place when and how they should with our limited and incomprehensible involvement. I admit, I've had doubts recently about the "plan" of my own life, wondering if what I'm doing is what is supposed to be done, if the waiting is necessary or a waste of time. I sit here thinking of you, my Love, hoping I'll see you in person, hear your melodic voice, look into your boundless eyes, and reaffirm my affection for you.

A12 MONTHS WITHOUT YOU   Part 1

Until that day arrives, I'll continue to wait.
Thank you for being here again with me, 'J', my Love.

PAUL S. DOIZÉ

5/25

Hello my Love,

I write to you, unfortunately not from *A12* but a booth connected to my side of it. Before my arrival here, I was speaking to my neighbor who lives across the street. Upon my return to the house after my shift, I noticed her pulling her recycling bin from the back to the side yard intended for the street. Noticing she was somewhat struggling, I offered to take it the remainder of the way near her driveway. She then said her garbage needed to be brought to the curb and I offered to do this for her also. She then asked if I would be joining her in her house to talk, and not having intended to do so nor had any other plans, I accepted but would need a few minutes before to feed the cat. I then returned to her house and spoke with her in the living room for over an hour and a half. Not wanting to overstay my welcome but mostly wanting to be here writing to you, I told my neighbor it was time for my dinner and left her house a few minutes after eight o'clock. I then walked back to the house, having enough time to wipe off the filth I had accumulated at work, changed out of my uniform, and after making sure several times I had my wallet, arrived here. There were two things I was anticipating, one of those being here to write to you. The other, well it didn't take place as it was supposed to and will maybe be delayed until tomorrow.

I've reconnected with someone who was at the store while you and I were there. It began yesterday at my store when I encountered her mother and spoke to her for a few minutes. Of course I asked about her daughter whom I haven't seen and/or heard from her in years and was curious. While we were working together I admired what she was doing: working at the store, trying to balance an aggressive program, and maintain her employment as a clerk. I assumed once she completed the program, she would quit the company and search for a full-time position within her area of study. But according to her mother yesterday, that didn't happen and she remains with the company in a management position. She has also become dissatisfied with her life because she isn't married and doesn't have a family at her age. Although she's still a young adult woman and engaged again (her third time) she feels as though she's "behind."

I know how she feels.

According to her mother, the man her daughter is with is good to her, is in management himself (which is how they met) and sounds happy with where he is in his life. The woman I remember wanted to be with a man who had "drive," and "wanted to do something with his life." I could tell she had passion for what she was hoping to do with her life . This was the quality and characteristic I most admired and respected about her. In a way, it put us both on the same motivational "level," having the same desire to do more than we thought capable, wanting to achieve, get out of retail for good. But we both remained within that "trap." It took me awhile to figure out what I wanted to do, even if it was after graduating from college and losing my job after almost 12 years. Perhaps, at least from what I can determine, I am meant to "redirect" her to her passion as I was to mine. Maybe the Lord has reintegrated her into my life to do what He did for me. This would be a great opportunity to "repay" Him for what He did for me and it would be wonderful for her to do what I'm almost certain she wanted to do. I know you're probably thinking I would also like the chance to pursue a relationship with her, and although I'm sure she is as beautiful now as she was then, my hair has become grayish and my weight has increased. I am definitely not the same man with whom she worked with – the shy, skinny, naive kid who was too afraid to ask her out had he been given a moment to do so. She may not even recognize me if we were in the same crowded room and not want to have any affiliation with me. This would be a useless pursuit, especially for an engaged woman such as herself. And even so, I doubt I could cause her to change her mind about intending to marry him; I wasn't successful the last time I tried which I found out the day after the ceremony had occurred.

'J', I hope I have better luck with helping her find some peace or at least assurance in her life. I'm sympathetic to what she is experiencing and almost relieved someone else, her being the last person I would consider, is suffering the same way which I did. Of course, I don't take pleasure in her conundrum, but it is comforting to know someone with whom I was acquainted has the same thoughts and struggles which used to overwhelm me.

Thank you again for listening, and my thoughts were of course with you today, as well as my love.

A12 MONTHS WITHOUT YOU   Part 1

5/28

Hello my Love,

I speak to you again from a restaurant but unfortunately from a booth connected to 'ours', also known as *A11* to the staff here. *A12* was occupied, and willing to wait for it, I noticed the young couple was either at the beginning or middle of their meal. At least I have a nice view of the outdoors, although the view is mainly of vehicles in the parking lot and the dry-cleaning place about 100 yards from my current location. Thankfully, there is sky and trees although they are somewhat obstructed by lampposts. The blue-gray backdrop is offset by the patches of pink, or perhaps it could be the other way around. Nevertheless, it's one of the most beautiful sites I've seen today.

But it cannot compete with your image at the top left of this page. How I wish you were here in person to enjoy this with me, but I realize at this time it's impossible. I doubt your husband would permit such an occurrence. The lights on the posts, at their designated time, illuminate the darkening sky, the trees becoming silhouettes against the blue-gray curtain.

Soon the trees themselves will disappear and become almost indistinguishable from the night sky.

I was called into the store manager's office today, having been forewarned about the meeting occurring at some point during my shift. Upon entering, I noticed the co-manager trainee already seated to the right and the manager behind his desk. Given the current situation in my department, I had somewhat of an idea as to the purpose of this gathering. I won't bore you with the details, but they wanted to make sure I was aware of the changes in management within my department and new people would be hired to replace them. Also, they were happy with my work and especially my attitude, but because business was slow, I would be unable to have the overtime I was looking forward to earning. But what I can only surmise as to the overall intention of the meeting was to inform me once the new location opens, I will be considered for a higher position in which I will be overseeing people within a department.

I have become a member of the manager's "club" which will hopefully cause me to be treated as a "friendly" rather than an enemy.

The meeting was then concluded with my shaking hands with both men and then my exiting the room. In total, the discussion lasted four minutes. Both of my supervisors within the department asked me if I had been offered the assistant-department-manager position which I replied, honestly, 'I hadn't.' I preferred not to tell them the specifics and instead informed them management was happy with my work, I wouldn't be allowed to work past 40 hours this week, and should probably take a "lunch" in order to remain there as long as possible. So at about one o'clock I went to the "steamer room" with a book, a to-go tea I had received from a local restaurant where I had recently dined, and a box of chocolate-chip cookies and sat on an overturned plastic tub to read for most of the half hour except for the final five to six minutes of it in which I took a brief nap. I then arose, returned to work, and continued doing so for two and a quarter hours until it was time for me to leave. And no, I didn't go over 40 for fear of having to explain the reason to my department manager the next shift I was scheduled with her. She owes me, or at least shouldn't be saying anything negative considering I worked her shift during which the president of the company arrived without warning and we had to make our department look presentable. Today, the manager told her it would have been "professional" to tell him of what she was doing because of this being a "professional" environment. She probably didn't care since her days at this location are few while having to take orders from this man of little or no concern to her which, honestly, I can't blame her. The assistant-department manager is doing his best to hold on until his employment ends, this man who was working today with a 104-degree fever, having a deeper voice than usual, and according to him, "drowning." He told me earlier he doesn't recall cutting some steaks yesterday he found in the cooler, but it may be because of me having done the task rather than him. I can't believe even in his condition a company would force him to work knowing his illness could spread among the staff and worse, transferred to the customers via his handling of the product. I would be surprised if, taking into account what he was made to endure, he would reconsider his decision to end his employment here, not only admiring but respecting his choice. This is probably why I decided to make him aware of what I attempted to do several months ago to the DM (district manager) by trying to "fight the good fight" but doubting "David would defeat Goliath" in this battle.

It's half an hour past their closing time and I think the family of three seated behind me and I are the only ones remaining. I better go ahead and call it a night in order for them to shut down and enjoy the remainder of their evening.

Thank you again for listening, my Love.

PAUL S. DOIZÉ

6/1

Hello my Love,

I write to you once again from 'our' restaurant and fortunately this evening, from 'our' booth. My entree has arrived and although I'm hungry, I'm not ready to eat it. I'd rather wait a little while, put a few words here, and enjoy the moment, even if you aren't with me. But you are on my mind and in my heart, and for right now, it's enough for me.

I began "officially" writing my story for the contest earlier today. It's unusual, but I feel as though I've written this story many, many times, yet when I put the tip of the pen to the paper it's as if I'm doing so for the first time. Once I began to move my fingers, the ink pours out and creates a letter or symbol, then either another letter or moves slightly to the right to indicate a space in between or begin a new sentence. Each word, even the ones containing a single letter, advance the story or communicate something to the characters themselves or as dialogue to another character. I admit, I don't feel as though I can't write a conversation, preferring to advance the story with actions rather than with what the protagonist says. So far in the story, it is progressing with mostly both characters speaking to each other. Neither of them is the narrator, and although I feel as though it's lazy, the person telling the story is an "all-knowing observer" who can even listen in on the characters' thoughts and accurately interpret their expressions. I had considered telling the story from the perspective of one of the characters but I would feel as though I was depriving the other "cast members" of the importance of their involvement making them appear trivial and as if they didn't matter. With so few people mentioned, each one has a specific "role," a set of tasks, an invaluable function no one else in that "scene" could do. Each person has their own unique thoughts, feelings, background, origin, memories, perspectives, interpretations, reactions, and voice. I want to give them the chance to be the person he or she was meant to be, to have a "life" of their own, to "live" to their full emotional potential.

They deserve and have earned it simply by their creation.

The two characters present are the only ones there are at that moment and are irreplaceable. I feel as though I have a "connection" with them, I "know" them, they "could be alive" if I wished hard enough or if they possessed enough consciousness. One of the characteristics I've learned when writing a story, especially a good one, is the characters/cast members have to be genuine, honest, and relatable, "honest" in the sense of being "true" to their role. I would hope, through my words, they become people whom you can almost "touch" and what happens to them can be felt by the reader. I would want the reader him or herself to feel as though they are in the room with them, they can see and hear this exchange, and he or she didn't have to be present before the conversation began. It would be wrong, ethically, to cause the reader to excluded, as though they should have "arrived" earlier, should have had prior knowledge of the characters, or at least been somewhat acquainted with them. I admit, names are necessary to distinguish between characters, but when you look at it, a name is just like any other word: a set of letters arranged in a manner to designate something, or in this case, someone. But the "arrangement" doesn't represent nor define the person – it happens to be the name they were given at their birth to distinguish a person from another. This is something which has bothered me for awhile, especially whenever I happen to be with my immediate family. I am related to them by blood, but it doesn't mean who it is I am meant to become. My last name was given to me because of my relation and my first name passed onto me as it was for my father, his father, and his father. But I don't want to be defined by a name or what was done by those who lived and died before I was created. The two women, so far, have no past except the one with her recent memories. What happened to the young woman then affects her at that moment and her actions will then affect her future. The mother is just as involved, not only for exposition (making the reader aware of the situation) but as a "partner" to the action, helping the scene to progress, almost acting as a "presence" for the reader. I can almost "see" myself standing there, watching this conversation, but I can also see myself as the mother, sympathetic to the young woman standing in front of the mirror, wanting to do whatever she could to help her daughter, even if it was only to listen. I've learned sometimes the most important thing anyone can do for someone else is to listen which is why I believe we were given two ears and only one mouth.

Thank you, again, for being my "ears" this evening, my Love.

A12 MONTHS WITHOUT YOU   Part 1

6/4

Hello my Love,

I speak to you from 'our' restaurant, however from booth *A11* which is connected to 'ours' on 'your' side. What I like about this booth, besides its connection to *A12*, is the view to the outside and, judging from the cloud cover, we're in for a large storm. The lighting has been flashing, reminding me of when you once mentioned "heat lighting" which, from what I've noticed throughout my life, few people are aware of it and how it's created. The rain is now falling, as though it's in sheets, bombarding the warm asphalt which will later cause the parking lot and roads to have an eerie "mist" over them. I wish we were sitting here in this booth together, facing the windows, watching the "show" together while we enjoy our meal. Although you're not here physically, at least I can enjoy it while you smile at me from the top left of this page.

We didn't have anyone to close the department this evening so I said I would work two hours over my shift until eight o'clock which would meet my full-time requirement, make me appear as though I'm willing to help (which will go toward the amount I'm asking for during my interview for the assistant-department position) and would pay for my meal. Sitting here and writing to you was what kept me going and gave me something to work toward. The feast before me happens to be a bonus, something to show for my effort.

I met a customer today who happened to work at 'our' former employer a few years ago. It turns out he, you, and I knew mostly the same coworkers, some who are probably still with the company. We even happen to have worked for the same store manager and both agreed about one of his personal flaws of showing preferential treatment toward certain people. He told me the manager one time had called him by an offensive name which upset him and caused him to respond by saying, "F--k you," which is something I still wouldn't mind saying to him if I had the chance. But those would just be words, briefly satisfying for me and momentarily injuring him. It wouldn't be worth stooping to that level to ease the pain he caused me and the anger I have toward him. But it's in the past and from what the customer told me, that manager is no longer at that store. Perhaps he pissed off another person enough to cause him to be transferred to another location and a lower position. Maybe he called the wrong subordinate "an offensive name" and was reported to HR. It would almost be ironic and justified. And sadly, that wouldn't be enough to satisfy me.

It's raining in sheets again, falling straight down rather than at an angle as it was earlier. Thankfully it will relieve us from this heat I was momentarily able to experience during my lunch when I walked to my car to retrieve some covers I wear on my shoes to prevent me from slipping on the wet and soapy prep area while I cleaned it.

As for my story for the contest, it's coming along but has been difficult to write not because of the wording, but the characters and events being so close to me. In a way I, as the writer, feel like not only the narrator but a witness as well. It's as if I'm in that room unseen by the characters yet aware of the identities and information applicable to the event occurring at that moment. I can almost "hear" her thoughts, accurately "read" her facial expressions, "share" her emotions. She intrigues me the most in the story, the person to whom I hope some people can relate. Perhaps a few will be able to "see" themselves in her place rather than the male character who shows up later, the one who took a huge risk and "put his heart on the line."

Sounds close to home, doesn't it?

Well, I'm getting tired and I'm sure the cat is looking for his dinner. I have a special treat for him which has become his favorite.

I was just informed a gentleman whom I've known for awhile and noticed in 'our' booth has taken care of my bill. I'm still going to leave a gratuity and will make sure I thank him for his kind deed. Maybe I'll find a way to repay him somehow for what he's done for me this evening.

Thanks again for 'your' company again, my Love. I'll pay for your meal the next time, hopefully, when we will see each other in person again, maybe soon.

Good night, with all of my heart.

6/8

Hello my Love,

I'm here again at 'our' restaurant and, although I arrived later than I normally do, I was fortunate to be able to be sat at *A12*. Thankfully the restaurant isn't crowded which means the volume isn't loud enough yet for me to have to put in my earplugs. A young woman is my attendant so far and I've already had a chance to have a brief conversation with the young manager who is overseeing this place tonight. I've already written about this several times but nothing directly to you about it. I was able to complete my short story and submit it within the last few minutes before the deadline. I actually almost panicked because part of the necessary formatting stated in the contest rules read it "required page numbers," and although I could easily do it with one particular program, I wasn't certain with how to do it on the free one the man who sold me the laptop had downloaded onto it. The "help" menu within the program wasn't helpful because it directed me to a webpage on another site. With only a few minutes remaining, I considered submitting it without the numbers but assumed the judges may disqualify me for me improper format. But I did a quick search and found a page providing instructions explaining it easier. So with a couple of "clicks" on the same number of menus, the page numbers were included although it took a moment to put them near the right-side margin. Honestly, I'm somewhat concerned with what I submitted because when I looked at it, I realized the page numbers were not in the same/correct format as the rest of the document. There is a slight difference in the fonts when I corrected it but by then it was too late to resubmit it. So what will probably bother me for the next few weeks will be their disqualifying my entry because of not adhering to their guidelines in addition to the many errors I made because I didn't have time to proofread and edit it before it was uploaded. I assured myself whatever I had written at a specific time I would stop to review what I had. But I had to include a few specific details or else the story's events wouldn't have been "connected" which is partially why I kept going past that time. I also promised myself I would like to have at least 3,000 words to the story which seemed improbable because it took me a little over two weeks just to put down 1,600 words. So how could I almost double that in less than three hours?

    Well, I ended with about 3,200 words but neglected to include the word count which, again, may disqualify me. The limit was 5,000 words which is what I had wanted to achieve but Mr. R's recommendation of "brevity" kept repeating in my head. I have yet to review and edit it, even with a single and double-spaced copy I printed today, but I'm looking forward to not only "fixing" it, but adding onto it, hopefully getting up to the 5,000-word goal I had wanted to achieve when I first began writing it. There was so much to say, 'J', which felt like the pieces of it were "spinning around me" while I stood in the middle of the "hurricane" where I felt as though I was able to sit peacefully. Although there was a lot I could include and sadly a lot which didn't make it into "the final cut," I wanted to include some specific references, kind of like "sprinkles" on a cupcake. They don't necessarily make it "taste sweeter" but they do make it appear more attractive and "eye appealing." There were details I had wanted to include from the beginning, sort of like my own "signature" in order to set it apart from someone else and if particular people read it, they'll understand the references and feel "involved" in the story, as though it was an inside joke or "secret" between us. It could also be like being asked to come onto the stage during the performance in which you now have become part of the show. There are more of these references I would like to include and will try to do so during my "writer's cut" as I continue to add onto it.

Otherwise, I had an interview for the assistant-department-manager position today. The interview with the store manager and his new co-manager (the co-manager trainee's last day was either this past Friday or Saturday) lasted only about 15 minutes. They still have more interviews to do and said they'll get back to me soon.

Speaking of time, it's closing time for them here. Thank again for listening to me, my Love.

6/11

Hello my Love,

I feel fortunate to be here speaking to you this evening from this booth in this restaurant. Considering the high school graduations I heard took place today, I'm surprised I didn't have to wait to be seated. I just got off a 10-and-a-half-hour shift because, like last week, we didn't have anyone to close the department. I was originally supposed to "punch out" at six o'clock but was asked to stay until seven. But due to the amount of work needing to be done and staying to help the department manager when he thankfully returned, I ended my day at around 8:16 with 40.25 hours for the week.

I was asked yesterday by the store manager if I wanted the assistant-department-manager position. Standing in his office with the new department manager, I was told the job was mine if I wanted it, my duties starting Sunday, with a dollar more an hour.

I declined it.

He then asked me to think about it giving me until the

next day (today) to make a decision. While on the sales floor, he approached me and asked if I had made a decision. I informed him, 'An additional dollar an hour isn't enough and I wanted more.' Unfortunately he said he couldn't pay me that amount but I told him he would be investing in his career by paying me what I felt I deserved. Seventeen dollars an hour is what I felt I was worth, even willing to negotiate down to a $15 to $16 hourly wage in order to meet him about halfway. I hope so far, 'J', I don't sound as though I was being unreasonable or feel entitled to a ridiculous amount. A dollar more an hour was really the best they (the store) could offer me? I'm sorry, but I find that hard to believe. This store manager...I don't like nor do I trust him. For someone who was placed in charge of a store at his age I don't understand, based on what I've seen and heard from him, how he was able to be where he is, unless he "sucked up" and "kissed the a--es" of the right people. He's probably got his head so far up theirs' he can barely breathe. I <u>hate</u> people like that – those who have gotten where they are and what they wanted by "schmoozing" up to those in charge. That person, unfortunately, is the DM who is "connected" with the president of the company which of course means that there is nothing I can do.

This is a no-win situation. That manager has too much control, has it "in" with upper management, and is regarded as "the golden boy" of the district. He is untouchable, too protected, and immune from any discipline from his bosses. They won't allow him to leave to another company without giving him anything he wants, even control of the new store. This is an environment in which I no longer belong, one which has become too political and the only way to ascend within it is if you "know" the right people and are willing to debase yourself while pretending to be incompetent. These are things I cannot do because not only do they go against everything I believe but go against everything I was taught by my father whom I attempt to emulate and regard as my role model in how to be successful.

Although a lot has changed in the business sector since my father was my age, I still have faith the basic principles are still relevant and applicable: hard work, effort, effectiveness, productivity, professionalism, and of course, sacrifice. My father demonstrated these on countless occasions, influencing me in the employee I've become. I regard myself at least somewhat intelligent, reliable, involved, interactive, cooperative, and ambitious – all of which make me, what I feel, to be what a good worker is supposed to be. Sadly, these traits seem to exist in low quantities in this store manager or not at all.

Yet he still remains in charge.

I just feel as though I'm underappreciated and undercompensated. I know of what it is I'm capable yet I'm considered as simply another employee who works there. I've told that manager several times to look at my online professional profile in order to see my employment history, proving what I'm saying is true, yet he still hasn't. I wonder if he's concerned at what he will see which will cause him to become intimidated and then see me as a potential threat. I feel as though I'm talking to a brick wall whenever I have a conversation with him, and if I wasn't being paid, I would consider it a waste of my time. I don't know what more I could say or do to convince him or anyone else in that firm to at least give me an opportunity to show of what it is I'm capable and earn a fair salary for it, at least enough for that position. I feel as though I'm almost in the same situation I was in three years ago except the manager has changed and although I'm hopefully doing well in my current position they don't seem to care about improving their reputation and profitability which is seen by their limiting of employees like me. This is why we've lost about one to two employees every week since the new store manager's arrival; his arrogance and sh--ty handling of employees have caused them to want to work anywhere else because they know they will be treated and paid better.

But, as I was reminded again today by a coworker, "They [the company] keep building new stores," which as another former boss informed me, "has to be paid for somehow which comes out of labor." This will cause them to, among other decisions, be nonexistent in less than a decade.

Well, I'm sorry if I bored and frustrated you with work stuff. They're about to close so I should go. Thanks again for listening, my Love.

A12 MONTHS WITHOUT YOU   Part 1

6/15

Hello my Love,

I speak to you again, thankfully from 'our' booth this evening. I asked the hostess if I've gained a reputation with this booth which she responded by saying, "Yes, but a good one." I wonder how many times I've told the staff here as to the reason why I request this particular booth or if they regard the story as obsessive, unfortunate, and pathetic.

For the time being, I have your photo turned over so one of the sentences you said to me that day stares at me. The reason for the position of the photo is because one of 'our' former coworkers is sitting almost across from me with his wife and child. I'm concerned if he politely approaches me, he will see your image, ask me why I have it while he remembers you're married, and will tell your husband. Not only would I be concerned about his actions against me but especially against you.

This time yesterday I was at the local cinema watching a movie with a newlywed couple I had met and spoke with before the film began. I was grateful for their invitation and didn't feel like a "third wheel" as I have many times before. Given their younger age, attractiveness, and likely amount of wealth, I realized being their friend would be impossible given our differing social and financial status. When the movie ended, I thanked them for their friendliness and told them the following: 'What you have is something I have spent my entire life looking for. Cherish what you have and no matter what, be thankful you have each other.' Then I stood up, said my good-bye, and walked away.

    I cannot fault a couple like this whose futures are likely secure and will be filled with happiness, ease, and certainty. The wealth provided from their own families will be enough to sustain them, their network of family and friends ensuring they'll always have decent and simple employment, and they won't be deprived of any of their desires. "Settling for the minimum" will never be in their minds because of their higher class while I will probably remain underneath them and seen as someone who is in need of their sympathy, pity, and charity. Although I may be seen by them as someone of intrigue and curiosity, it is only because of their wondering how I am able to survive with the limited resources and connections I have acquired and possess. To them, I am an "animal" at the zoo or an "exhibit" at a museum – to be observed and pondered, or even a pet to be seen with for attention. "Look how they've taken in that unattractive, lower-class man," their friends would say amongst themselves, "See how much they are willing to do for such a disadvantaged member of society."

    I'm sorry my thoughts went in that direction. Lately, I've noticed certain people with certain traits are able to have better lives because of being good-looking and somehow constantly remaining "above everyone," appearing to never have any discomfort, bad luck, or misfortune. They don't have to work as hard as most people, having opportunities "thrown" at them, never having to worry about lacking money, companionship, and living below their means. They'll never have to know the struggles which have happened to me and I've endured, never be concerned with being alone, and will always have family and friends available to help them.

Their parents will never be embarrassed and ashamed of them because of what they haven't accomplished.

Although I wasn't scheduled to work at the store today my department manager contacted me to let me know of what he experienced and what he ended up learning about the "ad change." Reassuring him it should be easier when the new-assistant-department manger arrives in their new position, he surprised me by saying the person the store manager had reached out to had changed his mind and will probably remain with his current employer. So suffice it to say, it may be awhile until the department has an assistant manager which will make all of our jobs more difficult and burdensome. I'm almost hoping the store manager will approach me again but this time with a counteroffer or perhaps agreeing to my original wage request. I doubt the possibility of this occurring because of him having a reputation for being "cheap" when it involves labor, either because of the demands of his bosses or his own desire for a larger bonus. For the time being, I'll "stick to my guns" as Mr. R advised and do whatever is in my job description and no more without proper compensation. If the store manager wants me to be the assistant, he is aware of what it is I want and, considering our dire situation within the department, can easily remedy it by agreeing to my desired amount. Otherwise, we will continue to be understaffed, tasks will go undone, customers will be unhappy, and sales will fall. This will then go against him being in charge of the new location or perhaps demoted to co-manager. As I told him the other day and will tell him again, 'I am not asking for just a suitable pay increase – I'm asking you to make an investment in your career.' I'd even consider using my "book analogy" I rehearsed with a vendor yesterday and hope it would be enough to convince him.

The restaurant is shutting down for the day and the group next to me just paid their bill so it's time for me to call it a night. Thanks again for listening, my Love, and again I apologize for my complaining. Telling you makes me feel better and prevents anyone else from having to suffer through it. And it brings me some peace.

A12 MONTHS WITHOUT YOU   Part 1

6/16

Hello my Love,

I realize it's only been a day since my previous letter, but honestly I wasn't in the mood to eat at the house alone again. I was looking forward to a 16 oz. t-bone steak I've had in my fridge for the past few days but something caused me to lose my appetite for it, probably the realization no one else would be there to enjoy it with me. I suppose I could have done this at the house, but the environment would be quiet. Perhaps I'm just having one of those moments in which it would be better to be around people. Thankfully this atmosphere feels welcoming, void of any "screens," and reminds me of you. Sometimes I'm almost able to convince myself I'm waiting for you to arrive, you had to step away to make a phone call, or you may be delayed because of a task which had to be done at your job. But my mind recalls you won't be arriving, you're not a few feet away outside, and your husband is the person who awaits you from your job, likely with a nice meal he prepared for you. Not in the mood for another one of my "usuals" because of not being in the mood for another one this evening, I instead chose a dessert that is sweet and contains ice cream. A simple thing like a mixture of ice, milk, sugar, and flavoring somehow manages to perk me up especially when it's covered in whipped cream, chocolate syrup, and topped with a cherry. I'm somewhat glad I'm feeling this way – it proves my medication isn't causing me to constantly feel as though everything is okay when it isn't.

Our new department manager so far has a negative reputation among my coworkers throughout the store. One person in another department referred to him as a "jack a--" who came into her department and was concerned about the amount of ice they were using in one of their displays which took away from our seafood case. Another coworker said, "He doesn't appear to know anything about what's going on," while another is concerned my boss is "struggling." But it was what I noticed in the cooler this morning which makes me especially concerned: I found a "tote" and a half of prepackaged ground sirloin which had been retagged with four additional days than what was on the sticker on the tote in which it was delivered to us. What was meant to have a shelf life and sell-by date of today had been tagged with the 20th. When I contacted him to do the seafood order, he said he was going to make burger patties out of it but his next shift won't be until Saturday the 18th. I had to show the co-manager this, informing him I wasn't involved and had found it earlier that morning. He told me I was right about not changing dates on product and he would mention it to the manager. For the time being, I took photos of it, put all of the retagged packages in a tote, and wrapped it in cellophane with the words "DO NOT OPEN!" written in permanent marker. I then covered it with another tote so my coworker who would be arriving later that day wouldn't see it and cautioned him not to even touch it. The department manager texted me saying our distributor has been sending us product with "short dates" and the store manager doesn't want us to "discard product" and instead "find another use for it." At this point, it's common knowledge the store manager is trying to save money wherever possible – labor, product, and expenses – in order to receive a larger bonus for himself. And I doubt he will be sharing it with anyone else especially those whom he has overworked and underpaid.

When I originally worked for this company as a stocker at another location, I acquainted myself with people who worked in other departments. One day, I was told an assistant department manager was terminated because he was caught changing dates on product which extended the shelf life of the item in order to reduce the department's "shrink" and waste numbers. I heard it was difficult for the manager to let this man go because they were friends and I personally doubt they remained so following him no longer being employed with the company. Given the "bond' my department and store manager have, I doubt any disciplinary action will be taken. In that case, I'll have no choice but to report them to HR, especially with the co-manager saying, "We could all lose our jobs because of this." I feel as though this co-manager has become an ally in order to rid the company of this piece-of-s--t manager, one who has caused more turnover than I've ever seen because of anyone and who has made every worker there despise him except those who worked for him at another firm and have somehow been "helped" by him with their careers. The problem I face, like several months ago, is the store manager is connected with the DM who is connected with the president of the company. I'm still uncertain as to whether or not HR is neutral among them or if the HR representative can be controlled by the DM. Whatever the case, if nothing is done or the situation is swept under the rug to be eventually forgotten, then I will have no choice but to report both of their involvements in this and, if necessary, escalate it to the head of HR or another representative in another district for an objective investigation. This time, as like previously, there is evidence to prove my accusation. I don't expect to be promoted, given a reward, or even acknowledged for bringing this to someone's attention. This is a matter of what is right and wrong and for a manager who appears to be "immune" from any form of punishment to finally answer for the harm he has done to the store and especially those who still work there for the time being. He is a <u>bad</u> manager who doesn't deserve to be in that position because of his lack of knowledge about store operations and the impact of his treatment of people. A large bonus shouldn't be his motivation – it should be taking care of everyone underneath that metal ceiling and making sure the store operates smoothly, effectively, productively, and happily. Sitting in his chair in his office earlier today, telling the co-manager as to the reason why I made him aware of the extended-date product – it almost "felt" right, as though I could do that job a lot better than the actual person who currently resides in the position behind that desk.

But I don't want his job.

Once again, the restaurant is about to close and thankfully my mood and stomach are better. Thank you again for being here, 'J', and helping me to work things out. Somehow I feel as though you can hear me even though you aren't outside or weren't able to join me here for dinner.

Good night, my Love, wherever you are.

6/18

Hello my Love,

I wish I was writing this in 'our' booth and in a better mood. Noticing *A12* was occupied by a person/customer whom I've despised for over several years, I requested someplace quiet and away from people.

Rather than the six hours I was asked to work to close the department, I ended up with six and a half, having only a couple of moments to grab a sip of my beverage in between customers and tasks. About two hours of my shift involved cleaning up the messes and "projects" the assistant-department manager had failed to take care of when he left after a few minutes after my arrival. But this evening, my thoughts are about the department and store manager, two people I have no choice but to report for misconduct related to the usage of out-of-date product. Although I made the store manager aware of this while I was cleaning today, I noticed opened containers of the product with the 16th on them. I have a feeling the expired beef was put into the grinder, "run through" it, packaged, and then sold either in a tray to be sold out of the display case or made into product. I also believe the meatloaf mix, which is a combination of beef and pork, was put into the grinder and again sold/made into product. I feel as though I've done everything I've been able to do, told the right people, and yet nothing has been done. Those two men are connected, friends with each other, as well as the new perishable co-manager. I know I have to contact someone higher, such as in HR or LP (Loss Prevention), but I'm afraid it will be useless because everyone is connected to the DM who is "protected" by the president of the company. What is going on here with the ground beef is wrong and it feels as though no one is being disciplined or held accountable for it. On top of that, the manager himself is ruining the morale of the store, even putting me in an uncomfortable situation on the sales floor, embarrassing me in front of customers.

'J', I feel alone in this. I wish you were here to help me figure this out, suggest what I should do, support me through whatever occurs. But you're not here, my sister is overwhelmed with her own problems, my parents will tell me, "Just quit but to make sure you have another job lined up before you do," and the few friends I do have are too busy with their own lives.

Once again, I'm alone in this.

I look over at my phone on the table, wanting so much to call you or wish you would call me. I wish I could hear your comforting voice, tell you my situation, and you would have a solution, a simple one I could have easily come up with myself.

But I've already done that on my own.

I know what it is I have to do although it may not be the best or even the most effective answer to this problem. I can't let this go – someone is getting away with this only because of whom his boss is and their relationship. It doesn't matter he is a nice and upbeat guy – he violated a policy not one of just the company but the health department.

I just told one of the staff members about it and he affirmed what it is I have to do – I have to report it. As he suggested, "What if someone died because of it?" which is what it really comes down to: our customers. Even if I have to go to the president of the company himself, something must be done.

Because it's the right and moral thing to do.

At this point, I don't care if the manager apologized in a way for what he said yesterday. But I can't allow him to get away with it and simply just "brush it off." What he said and did to me yesterday was wrong and apologizing doesn't make up for it. Nothing was done to our former manager when he "called me out" on the sales floor that day years ago and, as far as I know, he was never disciplined.

I can't allow that to happen again.

As I told the staff member here, I have a phone call to make in order to file a report to cover my a--. I have to pursue this even it may lead to my losing my job. At least I did it for a right and ethical reason.

Thank you for being here in spirit, 'J'. Perhaps someday you'll read this and cause me to feel as though you had heard my dilemma. Maybe it will have worked out for the best by then.

Thank you again, my Love.

6/22

Hello my Love,

I am surprised to be speaking to you from 'our' booth this evening. Given how late it is and how crowded the parking lot appeared upon my approach I assumed I would be seated somewhere else, perhaps next to the group of loud and older locals. I didn't notice them in the other dining room or haven't heard them, so they have must taken the night off or they're delayed. Although that group isn't here there are still many people here, many of them within our age range. It's nice to be among this "youthful" energy, hearing their young voices, enjoying each other's company out in public rather than being online or texting. However, the group of Christians whom I've seen during my past few visits here just arrived or at least one of the two or three families who sit together.

 I wish I could report a successful outcome to my situation regarding the store manager, but as far as I can tell, he still remains employed in his position as well as my department manager. I returned the HR's call yesterday during which he told me he would look into and investigate the situation as to whether or not it was handled properly. I still feel as though the department manager should have been terminated for what he did as well as the store manager for not attending to the matter immediately. I suppose once again, everyone involved is so well connected no disciplinary action will be carried out and those involved will be able to keep their jobs. I hope I'm not sounding as though I wanted them to be let go; I just don't feel the manager deserves to be in his position given his attitude and treatment toward his employees.

I'm sorry my words are few. Although I was anticipating being here this evening, my stomach has turned sour. My head is also hurting perhaps because of stress or this is my least favorite part of writing – when the pen is low on ink and what I put here is almost illegible. The task itself almost feels difficult with the scratching of the needle tip on the paper, almost making my teeth want to grind against each other. I've thought about switching to a newer, fuller pen, but since there's still "life" in this one, I don't want to abandon it just yet. It deserves to run its course until ink is no longer distributed, no longer put down words, its effectiveness has run out. Anything can still be put here and still have an effect: a confession to a crime, an offer for a job, a signature to a contract, a reaffirmation of love.

Once again, I wish you had been here with me this evening. I wish I had been able to hold your hand in mine, feel the softness of it, look at the delicate curves, and notice the chipped-red nail polish on your fingernails.

Most of the crowds have left, the group of Christians did arrive and thankfully were seated toward the back of this area. Only a few of those locals showed up and were seated in the booth in front of me near the windows. I removed my earplugs a few minutes ago since the restaurant is almost empty and it's about to close. The only person within my sight is a gentleman who arrived about half an hour ago, seated alone, with a mug of beer with his dinner and has been looking at his phone. Instead of sitting at a table the Christians, due to the number arriving this evening, occupied a booth. The gentleman has now left, the manager has lowered the window blinds, and my tea is almost finished. It's ten minutes past the time they close which means it's time to leave. I can hear the sound of the brushes cleaning the floor of the kitchen nearby.

I'm sorry I wasn't more talkative this evening. Hopefully my mood will improve with some good news, preferably related to my short-story submission or my head being relieved. But once again, I'm thankful you were here.

Thank you again for listening, my Love.

A12 MONTHS WITHOUT YOU   Part 1

6/25

Hello my Love,

I had the pleasure to sit in 'our' booth this evening with my sister and nephew. They were here for 45 minutes because he started to become "antsy" which, according to my sister, meant he was hungry. The straw he was chewing on kept him occupied while we ate. The affection my sister displays toward him is more than I would have expected from her and I'm proud that she demonstrates her love for him. I had been anticipating being here, writing to you, and enjoying this "feast" I am still enjoying even after their departure. Now that they're gone and I'm alone once again, I'm sad they're no longer here, wanting to have them remain longer.

Since the sun has set more people have arrived to eat here. Coincidentally, one of my coworkers from another department is seated two booths behind me with his girlfriend or a friend of hers. There were two other menus at his table and I've only seen one woman walk toward him. Seeing she didn't recognize me although we've spoken before, I have to assume the woman is her friend. In a way, I was hoping he would introduce me to her friend which would hopefully lead to being involved with some new people, perhaps a friend or two.

My workday went by quietly, having worked from nine o'clock to about five with 30 minutes for lunch which consisted of my sitting in the "steamer room," eating a few cookies, and reading a chapter of a physical copy of *The Grapes of Wrath* while flies were walking on the floor nearby, I suppose, because of exhaustion and/or hunger. I was taken by surprise by chapter five of this novel which I finished within that half an hour, the images and dialogue still remaining with me even as I sit here thinking of you and wishing you were seated with me. My department manager told me he was aware of my reporting him about the ground meat I mentioned last week and at first he was angry with what I had done but then realized he was wrong and I was right. He also said he didn't listen to me even though I had said what I know I needed to say to which he admitted he should have listened.

Side note: my coworker's girlfriend just arrived, to whom I greeted when she walked past me on the way to his booth.

Continuing...unfortunately he had to end his shift at 11:30 and my other coworker wasn't due to arrive for three hours. So, yet again on one of our busiest days of the week, I was left to work alone with only a few moments of assistance from either of the two co-managers on duty. I managed to make our "fresh-meat" section look better, enough to receive a compliment from the perishable co-manager. The other co-manager was attempting to set it up with according to a "plan-o-gram," but given the items listed on the diagrams versus what we had in stock, it seemed as though he was making it more difficult than it should have been. The rest of the store felt relaxed probably because of the store manager not being there which was a personal relief to me not having to be concerned about him showing up in the department randomly and telling me what I already know I need to do. The coworker sitting behind me now would probably agree with my observation and likely dislikes that man as much, if not more so, than me. Yesterday, the manager came into the prep area and told me to do something of no relevance or importance at the time. As he was walking away, I called him an "a--" aloud, almost afraid he had heard me. That man is the prime example of an "a--" who has more than likely "kissed" enough of them to be where he is. I even went so far as to fantasize about being seated directly across from him in his office, standing up, walking a few steps toward him, leaning down to where my face was almost directly in front of his, our eyes locked, then I open my mouth and intently say, 'You're an a--.' I then stand up straight, walk back, and return to my chair while he processes what he was just told. I just don't understand how a store manager does not work on the busiest day of the week which also happens to be the one some employees are having to leave early to avoid overtime. Before I left the store I noticed the lights in the bakery department were off signaling no had been back there for awhile to activate the sensor. Meanwhile, I heard from an employee near the "self checkout" telling another employee to say to anyone who asks about employment, "We are not hiring at this time because we don't have enough hours." The reason for this is obvious and I hope he enjoys whatever bonus he receives because of the inconvenience and stress put on us.

Well, my coworker and the other people who had been seated with him have just left and it's 40 minutes after their closing time so I suppose it's time for me to leave. Thank you again for listening, my Love, and making me feel less lonesome after my sister and nephew left earlier. Good night.

PAUL S. DOIZÉ

6/29

Hello my Love,

This evening I write to you, once again, from this restaurant but in booth *A11*. 'Ours' was occupied upon my arrival with an older couple and their son about our age appearing as though they had just begun eating their meal or were in the middle of it. As I write this, the three of them have departed but I do not regret arriving as early as I did or else I doubt would have been seated in a place near the booth behind me. At least from here I have a nice view of the windows: the clouds moving from right to left, "Unfortunately those that had deprived this area earlier of rain," according to my next-door neighbor. The temperature has lowered providing us with some relief from the summer heat, yet I was still sweating while I had the bedroom window open. Darkness seems to be descending soon although it could be due to the tint of the windows. If I concentrate hard enough I could almost pretend a mountain range, rather than a parking lot, is on the other side of the seat in front of me and under the treetops.

Like last Wednesday, I was scheduled to begin my shift at seven o'clock this morning even though my shift last night didn't end until 9:30. Upon my arrival at the store I began organizing the sale tags by their area and then applied them to the shelves. Surprisingly it only took an hour and a half which then led me to the arduous and inefficient task of altering the sales stickers on fresh product to now show their new discount and price. I began with the trays of pork, moved onto the ground meats, and was about to alter the beef when the store manager arrived in the department and began pointing out areas looking as though they needed attention.

My Love, I wanted to punch that man in the face for the amount of items he wanted completed, things of low priority and were in the process of being handled. All he kept doing was saying, "This needed to be fixed," and, "That needed to be filled up." My boss and I were already working as fast as we could yet it felt as though it wasn't taken care of quickly enough for this man who only said what we were already aware of yet this manager wasn't doing anything to help or offer any assistance to set the department up sooner. I had only been there for three hours, arriving earlier than this manager, and had completed what would have usually have taken about four to five for my previous department manager. This store manager has unrealistic demands and expectations while under the impression he is a good manager because of having acquired his position. But I feel as though the only reason he possesses it is because he "sucked up" to the right people, "kissing" their a--es, setting unachievable and impossible goals. The latter has cost him his reputation among his personnel who dislike, even as much as hate, him because of how he treats those he oversees. I assume he realizes the increased amount of turnover we've had since his arrival is because of him but because of his incompetence and demonstrated inability to comprehend what are otherwise basic concepts of management, it's doubtful he can make the connection. Given his displayed level of intelligence, or lack thereof, I just don't see how he has been able to achieve his position within the company with his skills and knowledge. I still conclude the DM (district manager) needed someone who wasn't as smart as him, someone whom he could easily control and manipulate, someone who wouldn't be enough of a threat to argue with or replace him.

I think I figured it out. I wonder if he is even aware of it.

'J', why do I constantly have to be supervised by these sh--ty people? Why can't I be under a person who could teach me, appreciate me, and treat others and myself with some decency? Is it too much to ask? But then I realize the sector in which I'm employed and it doesn't really attract the best and brightest people unless they're in corporate or upper management. Particularly in a self-advertised employee-friendly company such as this one, it's deeply political, connected, and difficult to be promoted or reassigned somewhere else unless you happen to know someone or have been accepted into one of their "exclusive" groups. I feel as though I was invited into one of these during a conversation I had with the manager several weeks ago when I was offered the assistant-department-manager job and then was told when the new location opened I would be in a position to have one of the "lead" roles which would become available. Of course, he is under the impression he has been guaranteed a place in the company in which he can make such a thing happen when I've overheard other older, more experienced managers will be applying to be put in charge of it. I suppose I'm overthinking this, should accept I'm in the wrong industry, and instead look for work in an area valuing intelligence, original thinking, innovation, experimentation, research, creativity, ethics, morality, fair treatment, honesty, and of course integrity – the same characteristics with which I was raised and taught to value. Sadly this store manager doesn't show he possesses many of those yet he doesn't have to be concerned with losing what he has. If I'm provided with the opportunity, I would like to pose the following question to him: 'Years from now what would you want us, your subordinates, to say how it was to work for you?'.

A department manager was terminated today and I can probably conclude what it is he/she will tell anyone who asks him/her that question. I'd like to ask one of the people whom my father supervised at his facility that question but I probably already know the answer which is favorable.

It's almost closing time here and I think I'm the last one remaining. I'm sorry for burdening you with my work problems again, and as always, I thank you for listening, my Love.

PAUL S. DOIZÉ

7/2

Hello my Love,

This is the first time I've been away from the house today, beforehand stopping by the store to check my schedule for the next few days. Fortunately I don't have to work tomorrow and, taking into account today, I have the weekend off the last time this occurring I cannot recall. But I do have to return on Monday morning for the holiday which I don't mind if it provides me with two consecutive days to recuperate, relax my body, be allowed to be my "true" self a little while longer than usual.

Assuming the restaurant where I've already had breakfast three times this week would be crowded this morning, I slept late, awaking after nine hours in order to "recharge my battery" especially after having worked five consecutive days which is unusual for me. After having a cinnamon roll while checking what was happening online in the world I brought my materials and tools outside and worked on my model kit until it was time for me to clean the styrene shavings and sweat off of my face and arms in order to be presentable for dinner here, thankfully, in *A12*.

I've been a little upset this evening, 'J', not only because of not having my story win the contest nor it being one of the six entries in that area to be chosen to be included in their printed literary magazine, but because of the loneliness which has been with me, the reminders of it upsetting me. My neighbors across the street were apparently having a party in their backyard pool, the sounds of it which I could hear from the carport where I was working. Vehicles were regularly pulling up to their driveway, parking on their lawn, and sometimes departing for a little while and returning with beverages. A gentleman at one point arrived in a car the same color, make, and model as yours I used to ride in when you used to take us for lunch up the hill from the store. For a brief, exciting moment I thought it was you showing up to visit me...

What saddened me was not having been invited to their gathering even though we haven't met. It would have been nice to at least be asked although I would have declined their offer because I would be a stranger to the other attendees. Seeing those people, the happiness on their faces, hearing an acoustic guitar being played, smelling whatever it was being cooked on their grill, and I'm several feet away, like a kid watching his friends play while he is inside because none of them even realize he exists. The only phone calls I received were a "robo call" and earlier this morning one from my sister who was crying because she wanted to be with her children who were with her husband in a city an hour away. Suffice it to say, I wish I could have been contacted by someone who wanted to have a conversation with me.

I told my father the other day I have "bad luck" which is why I feel as though nothing is improving in my life. While I have been telling myself since yesterday my story submission was incomplete and far from the decent work of which I know I'm capable, I would have been overjoyed and concluded my luck had <u>finally</u> changed. Even inclusion in their magazine, my entry out of 58, I hoped would have gotten someone's attention and put me on a path leading to a better financial situation with an occupation and far, far away from the store and that a--hole of a store manager. I was wanting to continue to tell 'our' story while a publisher would advance me the resources to sustain me while I completed it, seeing my true potential, knowing my words will want to be heard among those whose commentaries, columns, and opinions are published online. I was thinking this would "launch" my writing career and sincerely believe this would be proof I could show my parents I am meant to be a writer. But then again, I wish I would have heard about the contest sooner and hadn't been scheduled to work at the store on the day it was due in order to add more onto it and have someone, like Mr. R, proofread and critique it. I think now I've been away from the story long enough I should return to it, make it how I envisioned, perhaps in time to be able to read it to you in person.

 Well, my Love, I'm getting tired and I should call it a night. I was afraid after losing the contest I wouldn't have the desire to write anymore but in a way you encourage me which is why I'm here this evening. And for that, 'J', I am truly grateful for your inspiration and your smiling face at the top of this page which has been keeping me company even though I felt the world had forgotten I existed.

7/6

Hello my Love,

I greet you from this restaurant again although from booth *A13*. Had I arrived about five minutes earlier, I may have been able to sit in *A12*. But I didn't want to arrive too early, not because I may have to wait, but for the crowd to dissipate. Only about five of the booths around me are occupied, well now six, and the background music isn't playing through the speakers. Although I don't hear many conversations, I decided to go ahead and put in my earplugs anyway; it gives me a little "personal" peace and quiet.

The pen I'm utilizing right now, being the same model I've written with for over five years, is the last one of these I possess. A few months ago realizing I needed to restock my supply the retailer from which I've purchased a box containing a dozen never updated their website to show this particular pen was unavailable. Contacting the retailer directly led to my calling the manufacturing representative who told me the news I had feared: "The model of this pen was no longer being produced." Having passed by the twin pack of these in 'our' former-employer's-school-supply aisle whenever I would do the "safety walk" several times a day was what had caused me to purchase them originally, an item, in my view, was expensive for two pens when I could have bought an entire pack of cheap ones for the same price. But if I wanted to commit to writing I knew I needed the right "tool" to do the job, distinguishing it from other words I may put down on paper, appearing meaningful and important to me. I have enjoyed the smoothness of these, the needle tip as it applies its ink onto the page, the swiftness as it passes from left to right, fortunately able to keep up with my thoughts. But I realize it's not the pen that is the main component and origin of whatever I put here but the "instrument I play" to create these words which become "lyrics" originating as thoughts, ideas, opinions, and most of all, feelings. I've already chosen a new model and manufacturer of pen which to use, similar in design and hopefully compatible with the cap I showed you which contains the marks I cut into it whenever it has exhausted its supply of ink. If not then I'll begin with a new cap and allow my hands to form around this design. Then I'll search for one fitting my personal standards in a writing tool, possessing qualities which I described above, in addition to being reliable, affordable, and feels so "connected" to me I don't think of it as a separate item. It has to be part of me, an extension of my mind, arm, hand, and fingers.

 A month has passed since I turned in my entry to the writing contest, the one in which I lost, not even having the story being one of the six which will be included in their literary magazine. It turns out my submission was one of 58 in that particular category, far more than I considered. I am not angry or saddened by my loss anymore and honestly this is the first time I've thought about it since I received the message last Friday of winners not containing my name. I'm somewhat surprised there were as many entries as there were, my assumption being perhaps 10 to 15, maybe even 20, providing me with a decent chance of winning and standing out among the others. What I suppose consoled me was Charlie Chaplin once entered a "Charlie Chaplin Look-Alike Contest" and came in third place when he obviously should have come in first. This reminds me even one of the greatest actors who became famous without saying a word and relying on physical comedy rather than speech was still unrecognizable as being the actual person. Given my long run of bad luck and rejection I could have saved $15 and a month's worth of anticipation and excitement by not entering the contest at all, but I would have had to live with the regret wondering, 'What may have been or what it could have led to?'. The disappointment, as I've probably mentioned here before, is temporary and can easily be dismissed. The entry fee was a gamble, a risk I was willing to take, hoping the return would be larger than the investment, losing obviously being a possibility if not an inevitability. But that's how my life is – with loss, after loss, after loss, one of many of a long string of defeats, disappointments, rejections, and rationalizations. 'The money is immaterial,' I tell myself, 'What I would have spent on a meal or a few days worth of groceries in one transaction.' I then follow it with, 'I can earn the amount back in no time, thinking of it as part of the vacation/personal hours the company gives me which is somewhat of a benefit even though I had to work in order to receive it.' In a way, I do feel as though I gained a lot more from the experience by learning about myself, how dedicated I can be to achieving a goal, and what I'm willing to do in order to accomplish it, even deprive myself of sleep. I wish I would have had that mentality while I was in college but I was immature and didn't take it seriously because I lacked interest and passion during the endeavor, regarding it as something I was being "forced" to do. In a way, I did make myself adhere to the contest deadline, pushing my physical and creative limitations, adhering to a schedule with time having to be spent working at my job when I wasn't writing. Of course I could have "called out" for my shift the final day for submissions but the cost would have been higher than the entry fee. I wanted to somehow demonstrate to the Lord my level of dedication, was willing to do what had to be done aside from the story, not wanting to sacrifice a job guaranteeing compensation if I at least showed up and appeared to work. And I know I could have made the story more "cohesive" by reaching the maximum-word-count limit but I was able to double the amount of those I had in less than three hours. I do wish I would have known about the contest sooner, having had two months to create it rather than a little over two weeks. What I finished with is not my best work, not something I put my complete heart and soul into, not what I would consider as being "complete" and instead a "framework" which will require additions and "retooling" in various areas. I have to extend my personal appreciation to Mr. R for being my "spotter" during the process, in a way causing me to "stay with it" and not deviate or consider abandoning the path. Maybe this time, I will be able to ask him to proofread, edit, and critique it before I consider it finalized. And that's the copy I hope to give to you.

It's about 15 minutes after their closing time so I should probably go. I hope I didn't bore you and attempted to avoid talking about my job at the store. There is more to my life aside from what I do for about 35 to 40 hours each week like the other hours doing what I prefer: writing to you.

Thank you again for listening, my Love.

7/9

Hello my Love,

I write to you once again from this restaurant but from booth *A11* since 'ours' was occupied. Had I been a few minutes late, I may have been able to sit in *A12* because the diners there departed a few minutes after I was seated. I don't mind the view, however, from where I am sitting now, not only of the outdoors but looking at the people coming and leaving the restaurant.

My shift began at eight o'clock this morning but within seconds of my walking inside the store manager approached me, as though he was awaiting my arrival from his office. He asked me to "take care of the wall" as soon as I "punched in" which I did while the department manager set up the display cases.

I'm sorry, my Love, my mind isn't on this right now. There is a fire truck outside that was called because about 10 to 15 minutes ago an elderly woman was walked out to the patio with two of her companions. Either she was choking or vomiting but it caused enough concern to have the manager and a few other visitors involved. She is now sitting outside in a chair near the entrance where the crew of the fire truck is probably attempting to assist her. My heart goes out to her even though it was an interruption to my dinner. But then again, the fatigue from which has been bothering me ended this meal before it began. I'm just so tired from talking and although I was left to cover the department by myself for five and a half hours the store manager and his co-manager showed up only <u>once</u> to tell me what I knew needed to be done and didn't bother to help me. He was told by my supervisor I was alone and could have used some help but instead he probably sat in his office and then was able to take his lunch whenever he wanted. I'm not as angry as I should be because yesterday I was told his boss, the DM (district manager), the one whom I reported to HR is no longer over our store. This means the store manager's "friend" will no longer be able to cover for him, making him exposed and no longer "immune." When that man was arrogantly telling me what to do yesterday, under my breath I said to myself, 'Your days in your position are numbered,' and given our lack of foot traffic in the store today I'm certain it won't look good for his new supervisor with whom I'm on a first-name basis. I hope he is seen as the fraud he really is, corporate realizes he isn't the "golden boy" they assumed he was, and the only reason he's in the position is because he "kissed the right a--es" to get there. I'm not aware of the relationship between the new DM and the store manager but I hope it's one where he is regarded like every other manager in the district, perhaps more so because of his newness to the position. I can't say as to whether or not my report somehow caused his transfer, but I hope it was enough to get someone's attention. Perhaps someone actually took notice, investigated what I had suspected, and discovered some, if not most of it, was valid. That now means the DM's son will no longer be overseen by his father and assuming he too is not subject to his father's protection, I'm sure his position will be in jeopardy especially without being able to receive additional hours for his department, maybe even leading to his labor being cut like our location. Maybe he won't be able to sit at one of his location's computers sending off e-mails throughout his shift, the department actually requiring his involvement. Or he may just transfer to a store within his father's district. As for my involvement, I am still uncertain but would like to think what I did several months ago has resulted in something meaningful, I was right, and most importantly, my former-department and assistant managers were correct.

The woman was taken to the hospital because, as the manager of the restaurant told me, "She had something caught in her throat and the Heimlich maneuver wasn't successful." None of the other patrons complained but one couple seated near them outside left in a hurry. As I told one of her companions, 'My prayers are with her.' And again, my prayers, as well as my thoughts, are with you, my Love, and thank you again for listening.

7/17

Hello my Love,

I speak to you at a celebration I'm having for myself which I have invited you as my personal guest. I am celebrating not only my improved condition but most importantly my first day to eat out at a restaurant since last Saturday and the first time I've left the house since Friday. I can't tell you how I missed not only iced tea (which I won't take for granted ever again) but to be out among people even if I am alone, seated here in 'our' booth although it's on a Sunday evening. I wanted to dine somewhere I would feel the most content, the service would be good, and of course I could write in peace, not to mention I would not have to wait too long for more tea. Aside from the almost four-year-old steak in my freezer I ate for dinner last night most of my meals have consisted of baked-from-frozen hash-brown patties, sliced wheat bread, and warm decaffeinated Earl Grey tea I cooled with ice cubes. I realized last night the soda I was regarding as helpful to my condition was actually harming me, probably delaying my recovery. I suppose it makes sense the acidity of it has affected my healing and is why the pain of my throat didn't lessen. Having stopped drinking it yesterday afternoon the swelling has decreased and I can actually swallow without making a weird face afterward. This proves to me, once again, the importance of education and the idea of how "a person can never stop learning."

Typically after having an illness such as this one, I assume it necessitates a change to my lifestyle and/or manner of thinking about the chance I don't become ill again if not for awhile. This time I didn't think I would have such an "epiphany" but it was earlier today before my arrival here I realized what I needed to alter about my life, as though this illness was meant to "stop" me from what I was doing and cause me to reflect on the path from which I was deviating.

'J', thinking about the letters I've written to you lately, I noticed most of what I've told you is about my job, a subject which shouldn't even be mentioned here, let alone written about for you to have to listen. I've slowly made that store the center of my life, slowly moving it to the middle little by little while my writing is being pushed away from its dominant position. I suppose you could call it a "reevaluation of my life, taking stock of what is important, a rest stop on my journey in order to recollect, reorganize, and then plan for the next leg of the trip." In a novel I've been reading while I've been ill, a family was planning to move westward where they sincerely hope their luck would be better, the opportunities more numerous, and their fortune to increase. They realize what they've heard about this new area is based on pamphlets which, as the mother said, "Wouldn't have been printed at such an expense if it wasn't the truth [paraphrased]." My point, at least the one I think I was trying to make is like the family from the novel I just mentioned, they are going in a direction toward someplace they've never been with little information to give them some form of assurance their situation will improve. We are all on a journey called "life," going to places we've never been, encountering situations we're not prepared for, attempting to make the best of our situation. I honestly have no idea what will happen tomorrow because, as I've learned over the past five years, there are no certainties or assurances even when it involves our occupations, finances, and especially our health. What we can do, even if we feel powerless to everything else in the world, is focus on what is within arm's length of ourselves with which we can control. We can turn off a TV, ignore a cell phone, open a book, and learn something new by expanding our knowledge and imaginations. We can create worlds and beings with our minds, give them "sentience," and write about them in order to preserve their existence. In the midst of that "storm of creativity," we can find the "peaceful center" which is ourselves, feeling god-like powers which are at our command, being both the creator and destroyer.

All capable within our own personal capacity.

If I am no longer employed at my job tomorrow, there is nothing I can do because the decision was made before I sat down in the office. What I'm reminded of and needed to be again is it is a "means to an end," a method of survival, a way to get by to hold me over until something better and closer to my true passion is placed into my life or ahead in my journey by the Lord. What I can control is my perception of the world, its inhabitants, and its occurrences. I don't have to be upset and hopeless with my current circumstances — just accept them as they are and regard them as temporary. A cocoon may be seen as ugly and vulnerable but once it opens, a creature of beauty emerges from it, one which can take flight and travel farther in a shorter amount of time. I'm in a "cocoon," one appearing disgusting, below of what I'm capable, unattractive, undesirable. Someday when enough time has passed and the person has completed his or her transformation, an image of beauty will emerge, one who will be regarded as beautiful, magnificent, and wondrous. But it wouldn't be possible without the process underneath the chrysalis camouflaged to blend in with the nearby surroundings in an attempt to protect it from harm.

Maybe I'm more like a moth.

Well, I wasn't able to finish my celebratory dinner but I will have some to anticipate tomorrow. Thank you again for listening, my Love, for helping me to stay focused on what is important and within my control along my journey, and to a faster recovery.

7/20

Hello my Love,

I speak to you again from this restaurant but this time from booth *A13*. I just got off of work a few minutes ago and since I'm feeling somewhat better and having the desire to write, especially to you, I decided to eat dinner here even if this place is only open for another 45 minutes. I worked about seven and a half hours entirely alone and as I promised you the other day, I won't discuss my job to you except to say the alliterative nickname for the store manager, "(Name of Manager) Do Nothing," is becoming proven every time I see him while I'm working and he's sitting in his office only stepping onto the sales floor a few times in which he "makes his rounds" to each department and eventually arriving at mine to piss me off. And with that, I will not talk about today's shift.

However, I would like to tell you about a customer I met yesterday. I've actually seen him during almost every one of my early shifts and greet him like anyone else who I see in my department. But he has been returning my salutation equally unlike many other people when I encounter throughout the day. He is almost stereotypical for an older man in his late 60's to early 70's: gray/white hair, casual clothing, slight slouch, and utilizing the grocery cart to support him.

For some reason I am unable to recall, we began to talk to each other yesterday when I returned from lunch. He's from out of state, is a fan of the football team near that area, went to Catholic school, and taught English in a Catholic high school for a number of years. And what fascinated and surprised me the most is he is a writer, preferring to record his thoughts with paper and ink rather than using a keyboard and monitor. I still can't believe how much he and I have in common! I informed him I was just reading *The Grapes of Wrath* during my lunch and he couldn't believe I was actually doing this. I can't tell you how wonderful it felt to meet someone like him and share personal items about myself I can't with many people. It was almost like meeting someone whom you once knew a long time ago from a class or an organization and then found that person again years later, even if you weren't able to befriend, let alone introduce yourself to them – you both happened to be in a place where you had commonalities, the main one of being within the group even if it was random. Then you discover after the class is over or the organization is disbanded you all had more in common but were perhaps not having the desire to "get to know anyone" or preferred to stay with those with whom you were already acquainted. It's as if you missed an opportunity to speak with someone because you were afraid of venturing outside of your social circle or felt as though your preconceptions and impression of them was correct. But then you deprive yourself of the opportunity perhaps of them reading something you wrote or of something they wrote with the unique title of one of his stories which I look forward to viewing whenever I see him again. And if you don't mind, I told him I would provide him with a work in progress of the story I'm working on for you.

Upon us departing in opposite directions he said, "Speaking and meeting you made my year." I can't say I've ever heard this from anyone before, but it was nice to hear it, making me feel like a celebrity or a person of regard to another. I'd like to be that to someone someday, even if I'm known by only a few who know of my work but are unaware of my appearance. Then again, anonymity and obscurity has its benefits.

Well, its 15 minutes after and I need to get some rest so I can continue to get well. I'm glad I chose to come here this evening rather than return to the house for another dinner in front of the computer. It's nice to be social again even if my throat is still sore and I'm congested. It's worth enduring to be able to write to you again. Thank you for listening, my Love, and for providing me with some company, even if the seat across from me is empty.

A12 MONTHS WITHOUT YOU   Part 1

7/21

Hello my Love,

I'm sorry for writing to you again so soon, at least this time from 'our' booth. I wasn't scheduled to work at the store today but stopped by anyway to see the department manager whom I haven't spoken to in person in almost a week. Besides thanking him for working my last Friday when I was ill, I also wanted to check if I had left him with a decent "close" last night (I did). After picking up a couple of two liter sodas and a marked-down breakfast pastry for tomorrow, I returned to the house where I spent an hour online catching up on the day's events and if my coworker had responded to a message I had sent him congratulating him on finding a new job. He informed me he hadn't even started it yet and given his degree I told him I wish our company could give educated employees like us a chance to do more aside from what we do in our current positions. Attempting to not be online as much as I would usually be on my day off I put the computer on "sleep" and worked outside on my model kit for several hours. I did return indoors about every two hours to refill my beverage and check for any news updates or if there was a movie playing at the local cinema I've wanted to see, hopefully one I'd like to see again (there wasn't). Once I realized my thoughts weren't on my kit and I had actually undone several hours' worth of progress on it, I put it away, retrieved this notebook, and began to record my thoughts in the same chair but at a different location under the carport. A few minutes after I was seated and conveyed the lack of "heart" I had in my model, my father called on his return to his house to check on me and invite me to his home to eat dinner with him and my mother. Not in the mood to have stuffed bell peppers and preferring to be out among other people, I declined his generous offer and decided I wanted to be here in order to speak to you.

My Love, I have a confession to make: on the desktop of my computer, I have a photo I took of you, probably about seven to eight years ago. I think you and I were seated in the kitchen and I was messing around with my digital camera. You then posed for me to take a picture of you, your smiling-freckled face looking at me with some of your hair on the left side of your face partially covering your eye. You looked at me as though you were actually happy to be there with me and desired to provide me with a wonderful image, even if it was to make sure my camera was operating properly. I found that photo on one of my memory cards several years ago along with a two-second video I must have recorded at the same moment I took your picture. I have both of these among the many other thumbnails and icons on my desktop, I suppose in order to find these among the other files I have stored on it. I admit, once in a while I click on your image, eagerly wait a few moments, and then your smiling face appears on my screen appearing as though you are staring directly at me or we're teleconferencing or at least communicating face-to-face using our computers. But your image doesn't move and convincing myself the chat is "frozen" doesn't work or make me feel better. For me, seeing your beautiful face, the way I remember it from that time, is enough for me.

While looking at it today I began to think about the last time we saw each other: on that August evening almost three years ago. I then thought about how much your appearance has probably changed since the photo on my screen and the one you sent me from your phone about four years ago which I look at whenever I write, like I am now. Then I wondered how you may look now almost three years since I last saw your freckled face and if I would be able to recognize you if 'our' paths ever crossed again. Given how much has changed of my outward appearance, especially having eliminated my beard because of your dislike of it and the weight I've gained in the past year as a side effect of my medication, I'm curious if you would even recognize me, the youth of my face slowly disappearing and being replaced with indicators of age such as darker circles under my eyes and strands of gray and white hair among the brown ones of my sideburns. I suppose that is why I always like to be aware of whoever is near me, afraid of missing the slim chance you would be in town, preferring to remain hidden from me because of what was said that August '13 day. I've thought about that moment countless times, relived it in my mind more times than I should, convincing myself our parting words are why you've avoided contact with me, I remind you of the confusion and harm I caused you because of my selfishness. If any or all of these are the reason(s) and I'm not able to do so in person, I would want to sincerely apologize for any and all harm I caused you, whether it was a struggle you had within your heart, doubt I caused you about your marriage, or the sadness you felt when I was no longer your friend and instead another desperate, and potential suitor. I have and do feel guilty for the emotional injuries I've incurred on you and have asked the Lord daily to forgive me for those sins, even confessing them to a priest several times for my covetousness. I ask for your forgiveness as well and hope you will understand what I've done was because of my deepest and heartfelt love and attraction for you. And if I am ever provided with such an opportunity, if the Lord allows it, I would hope to offer my apology to you in person someday even if you won't grant me your forgiveness. In the meantime, I do ask you please also keep your eyes open for me like I do for you, be able to see the man I was those years ago, who hasn't lost my adoration for you. Please look for me.

Thank you again for listening, my Love, and for making me feel better about the burden I continue to carry on my soul for the manner in which I've treated 'our' friendship, the one I cherish close to my heart.

7/23

Hello my Love,

I'm glad to be speaking to you again from this restaurant but unfortunately from booth *A11* instead of *A12* because of it being occupied upon my arrival. My shift ended at the store about 20 minutes ago and, as I write this, I worked 40 hours this week, more than I was originally scheduled. I was told I could begin my shift two and a half hours later than I was originally set to because of my arriving early yesterday. While eating breakfast at the house I was sent a text to come in an hour and a half later instead which would prevent me from getting overtime, although I wouldn't have minded it. But I was able to put in for (4) hours of vacation time to increase my check while wishing I could just go ahead and use them all at one time but I suppose that's how it is with them. I am saddened because I was told the co-manager, who has been there even when I was employed there initially, is being demoted and transferred to another location in another city. I actually liked this man, even with his peculiarities and eccentricities, and admired his duration with the company. He told me, "It just wasn't working out at this store," which I then interrupted by saying the manager's name as the actual reason for his departure. He wouldn't confirm my assumption, but he did smile at me almost indicating my correctness. I will miss him and applaud him remaining in the situation in which he'd been placed by that manager, probably not one he wanted and certainly didn't deserve. What is disturbing to me is I knew at some point he would be "forced" to leave because of his mentality and approach to his job not aligning with the manager's. As one of my coworkers told me yesterday, "(Manager's name) is full of himself."

Well, enough about work.

I'm not enjoying my typical entree which has become my routine on Saturday. I assume this illness has affected my appetite by decreasing it to almost nothing except to constantly be thirsty. My right ear feels as though it has water in it and "pops" as if I was on an airplane. I've been sick for almost two weeks now and I'm ready to be well again. At least my avoidance of eating has seemed to cause me to lose some weight as far as I can tell. I'm still tired all of the time, weak enough to have caused me to take a brief nap before my shift even though I had been awake for over an hour. It has also caused my mind to create these unusual dreams in addition to those from the medication, having one so intense when I awoke yesterday I fell out of the bed onto the floor on my hands and knees. I can't recall the images and feelings I was experiencing at the time but it almost felt real. Maybe I need to take another day off to recuperate from this illness noticing sleep is the best remedy to be rid of it. I would hope it also takes away this lingering congestion and cough which has remained with me for months, an illness I was told "has to work itself out."

Before my nap, I was able to read a few pages from the book I've been attempting to finish over the past month.

Some of the chapters are brief, these almost acting like a "rest stop" away from the plot and going to another location away from the main protagonist. It's an unusual style of telling a story but a unique one in which you can "take a break" and look into the lives of a person or people in the background who are somehow "contributing," such as the waitress and cook who worked at a diner/gas station along Highway 66. I assume the protagonists will have some interaction with these characters at a point in the story but then again they might pass them by on their journey to California and both groups will never meet.

The reason I refer to this book is because of my appreciation of the style, Steinbeck's ability to build suspense and not boring the reading during the 400 plus pages of this copy of his work. It seems to be what is occurring in our own society – of having a short attention span, wanting everything right away, and unwilling to wait for it due to our lack of patience because of modern conveniences and a culture focused on instant gratification. It's almost as if the author could predict what our society would eventually become and had to make his novel adaptable and relevant in the years since its initial publication. Turning it into a movie strictly adhering to the novel wouldn't seem plausible given the length of the book but from what I've researched it has already been done. Wanting to avoid spoiling the story for me after I finish reading it, I'm almost afraid to watch a cinematic version of it. The journey of the main protagonists would have to be the main focus, perhaps not being eventful enough for a contemporary audience. I suppose that's why it's a classic and typically read in schools as an example of historic literature to reflect the time period. That is what I would like to write: a novel reflecting 'our' time period, accurately describing the circumstances in which we're living, the struggles we're enduring, the problems we face which are unique to us now rather than 10 to 20 years ago, a commentary or "voice" representing a majority relating to those who experienced certain events. Maybe that's what I should keep in mind as I write.

Well, it's half past their closing and the other diners are leaving which means I should too. Thanks again for listening, my Love, and to us hopefully meeting again.

A12 MONTHS WITHOUT YOU   Part 1

7/27

Hello my Love,

This evening I'm once again at this restaurant, but due to it being occupied, I am seated across from *A12*. A gentleman is currently finishing his meal, having been looking at his phone and is still doing so. He sits in 'your' place, attentive to his device while the seat across from him is empty.

My shift at the store ended about 20 minutes ago and I can't tell you how much I was anticipating being here, having a nice meal, and especially writing to you. I was scheduled to start my workday at one o'clock and upon my arrival into the prep area of the department I didn't notice anyone there. The hat and folded jacket of the department manager were placed behind the meat display case but there was no other indication of anyone else present. I assumed my supervisor was in a meeting or conference call and would be returning soon. The assistant was probably already gone because of his having to arrive early to switch out the sales tags and signs so I didn't expect to encounter him. I couldn't find anything written down telling me what I was supposed to do and concluded once the department manager returns he will inform me of my tasks for the day. In the meantime I cleaned up the prep area itself, washed items I would need to do so later, and pretended I would be shutting down the department soon. After an hour, he still hadn't shown up and I continued to keep myself busy. After two hours I asked the co-manager if he had seen my boss, his reply being, "(Store Manager's Name) probably sent him home early." So I had the department to myself and work the duration of it alone and without any communication of what it is he wanted accomplished. I did what I felt needed to be completed and in order to get me out of there sooner and make it easier for the "opener," the person who should have left me in better shape before he left today. But I suppose that's the way it is with me.

Alright, enough about work. I keep reminding myself I promised not to complain to you about it again.

The restaurant is surprisingly busy for it having rained earlier and lightning still flashes in the sky upon my arrival here. There is a group of Christians of a denomination of which I'm aware whom I see during most of my visits here. It's 20 minutes past the hour and I haven't seen them perhaps because they are seated in the other room, they haven't arrived yet, or they chose to eat somewhere else. Most of the people who were already here when I initially arrived and was seated have remained except the gentleman whom I mentioned earlier who was looking at his phone. I see a father and his "tween" son whom I saw last Wednesday and envious due to my father recently telling me he and I probably won't be having one of our meals together in the near future. After the last conversation he and I had alone at a table, I'm not surprised at his avoidance and appreciate he didn't provide me with a specific reason (other than the food at restaurants isn't good for his health) which may hurt or offend me.

I would like to take this moment and ask you a question,

one I would like you to ponder: 'When was the last time you felt alone, not just physically but also psychologically?'. Additionally, 'Have you been in a situation in which it was just you there, in the dark, with only your thoughts to keep you company? Did you ever feel as though there was no one else in this world who could understand what you were having to endure, no one in which to confide, no one whom you doubted had ever before been in that situation? How did you feel throughout it and how did you overcome it?'

We are all alone, 'J', whether or not we are convinced of it. I envy you in particular because due to your relationship status, you will never have to worry about being alone ever again. Your husband is always within reach or only a phone call away. And you will, because of him, never have to experience loneliness in your heart. To have a spouse in your life who loves you is who I truly have wanted for years. How fortunate you both are to have each other, to love each other, to cherish each other, to be there for each other. Loneliness is probably one of the worst feelings to have, a sense of incompleteness, emptiness, unworthiness, unwantedness. We all want to be part of something even if it involves only one other person; it's the association and commonality with the other individual which gives us some relief, acceptance, validity. We just want to be wanted by another person. But for those of us who exist without someone with whom to be complete, we continue on.

It's ten o'clock and the restaurant's closed. Thanks again for listening, my Love.

7/30

Hello my Love,

The only thing keeping me going today, to work nonstop upon my arrival at the store, to get out of there soon enough to have more time to enjoy this moment, was to be able to talk to you. That place...every day I'm ready to go up to someone in upper management and tell them what is actually happening at that store and ask what he or she plans to do about it. But it would probably fall on "deaf ears" or, as with my experience with the store manager, right over his/her head due to its complication.

But my thoughts are not currently of that place nor should they be. They are rather about a woman.

I have seen this young woman a few times and she always purchases a tenderloin filet from our department. I'm aware of this because I have assisted her several times and wondered why she doesn't purchase more than a single steak. I assume perhaps her boyfriend or husband and she were going to share it or he already had his entree and she preferred something else instead which caused her to stop by our store. If this was the case, I felt sorry she had to do it for herself and her "significant other" wouldn't do so. But then again, I look at a lot of women with these men and I wonder what it is attracting her to him. According to one of my coworkers, he answered it easily: "That guy probably has a large d--k," which honestly makes sense to me and allows my mind to move onto another subject.

Surprisingly this attractive woman appeared at my counter and routinely asked for a tenderloin filet. I showed her a few I had cut and packaged earlier which were close in size to what she requested a few moments before. I'm not sure why but my curiosity must have taken over and I began to suggest she purchase two of them, the other meant to be for her "other." She informed me all she needed was one, which I replied, "I guess your boyfriend must not be a fan of them." After a brief conversational exchange, I learned she is single because she had just gotten out of a relationship and wanted to take some time to focus on herself and concentrate on school. I then wished her good luck and she departed with one of the steaks to cook at her friend's place.

I could have asked her out. I wanted to ask her out. Instead I had the idea to try something different.

One of the characteristics I like about myself (not to sound vain) is I regard myself as being atypical of other young men, the same ones who are with these beautiful women who are attracted to one "thing" their boyfriend/husband possesses. I am accustomed to being rejected especially by women as pretty as her. I don't regret not asking her out on a date or for her phone number. I'm not disappointed I wasn't able to have a longer conversation with her. I'm not "beating myself" up right now for what I could have said or done.

I wanted to approach this situation differently.

Perhaps she won't think about it or wonder why I didn't immediately decide to "make an advance" on her. Maybe she will ponder what she may have done or said wrong: her low-cut blouse didn't expose enough cleavage, she wasn't direct enough, or assumes I'm not "into" women. She possibly may appreciate my avoidance of "pushing the issue" and I respected her decision to take some time to focus on herself. With each bite of her filet, she will repeatedly ask herself, "Why didn't he want to take further interest in me?". I wouldn't be able to regularly purchase steaks for her costing $21.99 a pound nor be available on Saturday afternoons to spend time with her and her friends. If she is still in college and wants to concentrate on it, then I admire her for having the patience to do so and at some point learning who she really is and wants to do for the rest of her life. I wouldn't feel right to deprive her of such an opportunity.

Then again, she may think fondly of me not putting her on the spot and being like all of the other countless men whom she encounters and ask her out. Maybe I'm the only one who hasn't "made a move" on her when whomever he is discovers she's available. I'm not concerned about what she thinks or what I could have done – I wanted to practice what and how it is I regard myself. And I'm proud I did, rather than feeling lonely because she isn't here. I said what I needed to say to you then and I don't regret it, especially if it has caused you to prefer to stay away because you are a married woman. I've been at the point, since 'our' encounter four years ago, I can't regret what I've said because it would be denying my heart and myself as a person. Being forthcoming and honest with those whom I love...that is one of the characteristics I cherish about who I am among the other "unique" parts of what I define as "me."

Well, it's half past their closing time and this middle-aged man on a date has been speaking loud enough for me to hear through these earplugs. Thanks again for listening, my Love, and for reminding me of something decent you somehow always knew about me, especially if I couldn't see or wasn't aware of it. Thank you, my Love.

8/3

Hello my Love,

I would first like to apologize for writing to you on this medium. I was dining at another restaurant last night and was hoping to spend most of the meal recording my thoughts and observations. I didn't realize until the beginning of my entree there were only three sheets of paper remaining at the time I had begun. I hate being limited by something so trivial such as not having enough paper or space to put my thoughts somewhere visually and if it had come to it, I would have written on paper towels dispensed from the restroom since the establishment where I was eating last night was "upper scale" and instead had their dinnerware wrapped in cloth napkins. I admit, such a place is somewhat too fancy for me especially when I feel as though I had to wear my Church clothes in order to feel appropriately dressed for the atmosphere even though such vestments aren't required in order to have a meal there. I just feel better "blending in" and abiding by the classiness of the environment in which they're attempting to portray, my attire signifying my appreciation for what their staff is trying to create, and my respect for their effort to maintain an appearance of upper-class dining and professionalism.

So enough about last night's dinner and onto the paper to which I am accustomed.

It has been a long and arduous nine consecutive shifts punctuated by this one which began at five o'clock this morning and ended at 1:30 this afternoon. The assistant-department manager and I had to do the "change over" for the new week and thankfully accomplished it easily and efficiently. The store manager made his "daily rounds of pissing people off," having become a joke between a coworker and I because of the manager criticizing the condition of his department before even saying, "Good morning," to us. I suppose that's one of the few ways to cope with the harsh treatment of this man – to make what he does and say appear humorous even though he himself takes it seriously.

The fatigue I had after my shift caused me to have to take a nap if I hoped to be awake enough to be able to be seated here and write coherently to you. The overcast sky, lower temperature, and eventual downpour provided a better setting in which I could rest comfortably while the cat lay nearby as though he enjoyed a "sleeping companion." It's unusual the three to four hours of sleep I can acquire in the afternoon is more effective than the seven to eight hours self-interrupted throughout the span of it in order for me to take a break, awake to have a snack, and then return to bed. Later I will arise, usually a few minutes before a shift begins and feel more tired than I was six to eight hours prior. I attribute this to my disposition toward that job preferring to have any other position at another firm but always wanting to write occupationally. In the meantime, until I'm hired by another company, turn in my two-week notice, and tell that manager how much of an a--hole my coworkers and I regard him, I'm "stuck" there.

    I had an interesting dream during the three to four hours I slept earlier: for some reason I had temporarily rented out one of the rooms of where I happened to live. I wasn't aware of whom the tenant was until his departure along with two assistants. It turns out the person who had stayed in the room was the CEO of a company who needed the room while he was doing local research. The CEO turned out to have some affiliation with my father who had made the suggestion to this friend. My sister had made the preparations for my "guest" while I hadn't made any contributions to his comfort or accommodations. I wasn't even told of who he was until he and his assistants were "checking out" and leaving the house, seeing them carry their luggage outside while I stood there in astonishment. I then began to confront my father as to why he never told me of his knowing this CEO and wondering why he had never introduced me to this person who could assist me with acquiring a position in his firm. Because I hadn't done anything to attend to my guests' needs, I appeared lazy and avoidant to this man who probably wouldn't even want to speak with me about a potential career. The CEO realized my lack of work toward his "stay" and ignored my requests to speak with him. Finally, after pleading to him for anything which could possibly emancipate me from this area, even if it involved me flying to another city, he told one of his assistants to get my contact information as they were about to get into their vehicle and leave.

    This dream, as unusual as it may sound, reflects how I currently view my life. I feel as though there are people withholding possibilities for improvement from me because I am undeserving to them in their eyes. There are also others who don't do more work than me and their achievements are noticed by those who show their appreciation and are in the position to help advance their careers. And of course there are the supervisors and corporate staff members who won't even give me a chance to demonstrate of what it is I'm capable and will only assist me if I lower myself to begging or making a scene in which they take pity on me and then feel unhappily obligated to help me. These, combined, all cause me to experience a sense of being "stuck" where I am, unable to "break the glass ceiling" above me, having to remain in a "cage" not of my own creation and forced to stay in there because of those undeserving of their opportunities and positions holding the "keys" to the "locks of the many doors" of which I would like to "pass through." Until someone feels like taking a risk and "unlocking one of those doors," I feel as though I have to endure the view of "barbed-wire bars" on all sides.

I hope I haven't saddened you too much this evening and I express my most sincere gratitude for you being here. Thank you once again for listening, my Love, and allowing me to convey my thoughts on what I feel is a desperate and impossibly-resolved situation.

8/6

Hello my Love,

Although it may have involved waiting about an hour to sit here in *A12*, I am thankful for the fortune to do so this evening. Upon my initial arrival, I was sat at *A11* which would have given me a better view of the outward-facing windows. I was curious to know who was in 'our' booth, perhaps considering waiting a little while if the occupant was almost finished with their meal. The person seated there happened to be a gentleman I knew from the store, Church, and had dinner with at this restaurant several months ago which turned out to be a wonderful conversation with someone who is a few years younger than my father. I have looked forward to speaking with this man (not the writer whom I mentioned in another letter) again and hoped our paths would cross again which is what occurred this evening.

I sincerely wish I could talk to my father in the way I do with this man: almost as equals. However, I always feel "lower" than him, as though his age and our relationship makes him far superior and he cannot "step down from his peak" and listen to me without causing me to convince myself I'm wasting his time and not "worthy" to have him hear my words.

I felt comfortable enough to tell this man about my reason for preferring this booth: the event which happened here between you and me four years ago. I also revealed whenever I do sit here, I write a letter to you. Out of curiosity, I assume, he asked me if you read them and sadly I admitted the length of the absence of being in each other's lives. I then showed him the physical photo of you which I look at while I write (the same one I'm looking at in this moment) and conveyed I look at you for inspiration, would want my writing to appear as though we're having a conversation, we are equals, and doesn't sound as though I'm wanting to sound "better" than you. I then reluctantly confessed if I die, at least these letters will tell you how much I thought about and loved you even during the long spans in which we didn't see or speak to each other. This is something I've told to only one or two others besides you, the others being people whom I feel would have some idea of how it is. My father isn't one of the few and I honestly fear telling him because of his habit of criticizing and belittling me for "wasting my time with such pointless things when I should be focusing on making more money and getting a better job." There are topics here in these words I feel I can have only with you, even if you don't respond, but somehow I know you can "hear" me and you will be able to read this someday even if I'm not there to personally give this to you. And there are things my family won't ever know about me but can take solace in reading the sentences written by their "actual" son, brother, grandson, friend, coworker, and subordinate. I can't regard whatever I record here, even if it is uninteresting and doesn't make any sense, as a waste of time. Words spoken by me can be thought of as lies when heard by my parents but I would hope reading my thoughts directed toward them would be enough to reveal who I really was. Thankfully I feel I was able to be that person to you.

The restaurant has closed and another booth of people and me are the only ones remaining. I should go ahead and call it a night. Thank you once again for listening, my Love, even if you aren't here with me in person.

8/7

Hello my Love,

I apologize it has been less than a day since I wrote to you, sooner than I normally do. I wasn't scheduled to work at the store today and promised myself I would enjoy my day off, a welcome respite from my recent illness. After attending Church, taking myself out to breakfast, and catching up on the news online along with a mid-afternoon nap, I spent about four to five hours outside working on a model kit. I considered progressing on what I've called my "ambitious project," but having waited over a week and still not having received the parts I purchased for $28 through a website, I wasn't really in the mood to advance it. So instead I became inspired by an unstarted kit which has been on my bedroom floor for a few months and decided to "take a break" and begin this one. However, I have had a couple others in my room I began over two years ago and would bring them with me when I was employed at an office to keep me busy during my many hours between clients. Sadly, once I went through my bout of depression I lost interest in all things related to model building and set these aside, untouched until several months ago. Although I only paid attention briefly in order to reorganize the container in which I kept them, returning to at least complete them has been on my mind even during this "ambitious project" which has occupied my time during the evenings I'm not scheduled at the store and feeling well enough to stay awake and focused. Assuming the website is legitimate and I do receive the parts, I will of course return to the other aircraft requiring a lot of effort but in the meantime, I'm hoping to take what I was working on over two years ago and integrate the materials, knowledge, and skill I gained and apply it to the kit I lifted up from my bedroom floor, removed the intact bag of pieces from the box, opened the box, and used one of my hobby knives to remove the halves of the body of the aircraft from the "trees." And with the initial cutting of the "tab," I feel as though I started another project, another journey, another opportunity to hone my skills, direct my focus, and keep my mind occupied while I also think about topics which interest me, problems I'd like to solve, the progression of my novel, and of course if you will joyfully surprise me again with your presence.

I realize the events of my day likely sounded boring and uneventful to you but there is another reason why I mentioned it which honestly I just discovered. As human beings, we are fortunate to be advanced in most areas compared to all of the other species of plants and animals. We don't have to be concerned with protecting ourselves by avoiding many predators who would hunt us for food. We can innovate, communicate, and collaborate if necessary depending on the situation. What I feel provides us with a distinction from most animals is our ability to learn and build on the knowledge we acquired through experiences. Imagine how humanity would be if we were born having all of the education we would ever require without the ability to add onto what we already possess. There would be no need for schools, libraries, or any tools able to expand our minds. The internet and publications would only be used for entertainment and because of that we wouldn't be able to advance. What if some people had more intelligence than others because they happened to be born in such a way? Would they be regarded as "intellectually wealthy" and esteemed to a ruler or deity? Would we be capable of adaptation and survival?

With each kit I work on and many of which are still in progress, I attempt to try a new technique or improve on one I tried on another kit. For example, adding electronics to a model to make it more "realistic" has fascinated me and I've tried to integrate a power supply for lights and a motor. Someday I would like to complete one having this installed successfully proving to me I could research, educate, experiment, and apply it. Coincidentally I like to think of it as the scientific method I learned about in elementary school and apply it here to advance my knowledge, building onto what I've learned. If there is one piece of advice I would offer to you and to everyone is, 'Keep expanding your knowledge by always wanting to educate yourself.' Don't remain "fixed" intellectually and don't avoid trying something new. Keep learning.

Well, they're about to close in a few minutes and I'm getting a feeling they want me to leave. Thank you again for listening even if it was so soon. And thank you for keeping me company, my Love.

A 12 MONTHS WITHOUT YOU   Part 1

8/10
Hello my Love,

I can't express how much I'm relieved to be here this evening. I just completed an eight-and-a-half-hour shift in which I, surprisingly, was able to take a 30-minute lunch, or rather was required to according to the co-manager. In order to preserve my "secret place" where I typically read during my "meal," I had to spend the 30 minutes in the lounge, a place where I used to go to eat my microwaved meals and sit and stare at the wall directly in front of me. Reluctantly I did so today except instead of an entree having cooked for five and a half minutes I had a box of a dozen peanut-butter cookies from the bakery-markdown rack. And instead of staring at the wall, I was continuing my reading of *The Grapes of Wrath*, or at least tried to. A few minutes after my arrival and about two to three pages read of the novel, a young woman who works as a cashier walked into the lounge. She politely greeted me which resulted in my returning the gesture and then took a seat in one of the chairs near the wall running parallel to the one which I was seated in front. I assumed our acknowledgments of one another would be the end of our interaction and she would have seen me reading causing her to leave me alone but she then began to ask me questions and discuss her experiences at "Bible Study." I tried to make it appear to her I wanted to return to reading but I suppose she didn't "get the hint." I seriously considered telling her I didn't want to be disturbed but I didn't have the heart to make her conclude I was rude or trying to be a jerk especially since she told me this was her first job and was still in high school. I didn't want to be regarded as "the guy who was mean to her" and was to be avoided by the other employees. Thinking my lunch was to end in a few minutes, I told her I had to return to work but before I left I said something I would hope would cause her to think about her future and she shouldn't allow this job to influence how she feels about every job she has after this one. As I was leaving she replied she "was only wanting to work here a year and move onto something else" which I returned by saying, 'That is what I said to myself too.' When I "punched back in" the time clock said I was early and still had 10 minutes remaining on my lunch. Not wanting to return to the lounge, I noticed the "receiving office" was open and sat in a chair in front of the computer to read my book for the time I had left.

I know I promised you I wouldn't speak to you about my job but I do so here because of "role reversal." At one point in my life before you and I had met, I was exactly like that woman: young, polite, out-going, talkative, oblivious, and energetic. Sometimes I would sit in the breakroom, even in the smoking half of it, and attempt to have conversations with coworkers twice my age and even older. I felt as though I had to always "remain in character" to do so. I also felt it was what everyone there expected of me continuously throughout the day and dropping that personality, even for a second, would be harmful to them and prove to my coworkers even someone like me couldn't maintain the charade forever. And you know what?

They were right.

Since returning from "meal" and throughout the remainder of my shift I thought about what I wanted to tell her, or rather, the person who I used to be at that initial stage in my employment. I pretended the person in that chair had been me years ago when I was employed after only a year, when I had become more extroverted and was a person who was entrusted with additional responsibilities. I will continue to think of that person, look at him, and reflect on how far I've come. But since this restaurant is about to close for the evening, those thoughts will have to wait for another time.

Thank you for listening, my Love, even though I spoke about work once again.

PAUL S. DOIZÉ

8/13

Hello my Love,

I speak to you once again from 'our' booth, having just completed a seven-hour shift which was originally only supposed to be six. I also speak to you on the eve of actions I know I will have to take, actions which may cause retaliation against me.

   I know I promised you I wouldn't speak to you about my job but, 'J', I realize of everyone with whom I am acquainted, you would understand the situation I'm involved. One of my favorite memories is one which occurred about six to seven years ago when I was managing an area at 'our' store. During one particularly stressful day (out of all of the others) you noticed how bothered and upset I was and told me to meet you near the nearby restrooms. You then motioned me to stand against the wall and you stood directly in front of me. Aware of my habit of not looking at anyone in their eyes, you told me to look directly into yours and to listen to what you had to say. Grabbing me on each of my upper arms you then told me, "Relax, it's going to be okay." Somehow your words affected me enough to go back to work and kept me calm the rest of my shift.

I can't tell you how many countless times, especially over the past four years, I thought about what you did for me that day and sincerely wished you were here to comfort me at this moment of distress, anger, and frustration. However, you did leave me with a memory I have revisited during bouts of wanting to give up and surrender to the direness and hopelessness of the situation. All I had to do was to remember the feeling of your gentle hands on my arms, the warmness of your breath, the soft tone of your voice, and the reassurance in your eyes as they looked and met with mine.

I've actually sat here, one of only two tables occupied in this restaurant, and seriously considered calling you in order to hear your voice again even for a brief second. But I immediately remind myself you are still married and I shouldn't think about calling a woman who is committed to another man especially if he ends up answering when I attempt to call. Also, I have to assume your avoidance of contacting me is your way of telling me we can no longer be affiliated with each other even as friends, colleagues, and former coworkers. As someone who said what he felt he had to say during both of your visits, I have to respect your preference to be left alone with your husband as your closest and only companion.

Sadly I'm the only diner here and they are closing for the evening. I can't tell you how much better I feel speaking to you this evening. Although you weren't actually here, all I had to do was look across the booth for 'your' company. Thank you again, my Love.

PAUL S. DOIZÉ

8/17

Hello my Love,

I have been anticipating being here this evening to speak with you while I was working my six-and-three-quarter-hour shift at the store today. Surprisingly there were many vehicles in the parking lot upon my arrival and I feel fortunate to be seated in 'our' booth. To my left at two tables put next to each other are members of my parish, most of whom I've seen but haven't been formally introduced. I know this may sound uncatholic of me, but I don't necessarily like them because they don't speak to me at the restaurants where we've both dined or invite me to eat with them. I'm sure they've seen me, are aware we attend the same Church, and yet don't uphold the values of fellowship and friendliness to other members. It must be nice for them to be able to "parade" themselves as "one-hour Catholics" every week and ignore those who worship with them.

I had a conversation with our store's DM yesterday which

didn't go well. I'm still bothered by it today especially when he referred to some of my words as "ridiculous." Since I've known him, I've regarded him as a decent man who was one of the few members of upper management whom actually knew what they were doing. I turned to him for assistance because I felt he would be objective, fair, and receptive to one of his subordinates who needed him. However, after the few brief moments he "allowed" for me to speak with him on the phone I now think of him as an arrogant, pompous, idiotic and self-centered man. If he had entered my department today, I may have punched him in his face. He is the type of person who this company needs to avoid hiring and retaining but doing the opposite has impeded them and prevented them from standing out among other retailers. They were so welcoming to this new identity yet kept the same personnel, especially upper management, throughout the transition. And these managers will revert to what it is they did before the transformation demonstrating this new appearance wasn't worth it and had no effect on improving the company.

'J', I know I promised not to speak to you about the "politics" I encounter with this job, but it's wearing down on me to the point I'm losing my self assurance that wherever I work will be employed and operated by at least somewhat competent people. What I've experienced so far has caused me to assume the people who are in positions I could easily complete the tasks are incapable of doing so. My conclusion is the only reason they still have their jobs is because of the friends, family, or acquaintances who are protecting them. What happened to the most qualified person having the job not the one most closely related? Had I known it was going to be like this when I was younger, I could have saved myself a lot of money and stress by not attending college. My degree almost seems worthless and my time there a waste when I could of instead been networking and, in the store manager's case, "sucking up" to the right people and allowing them to plan my career path.

I once again contacted he president of the company, this time to ask him for his help with this situation. I haven't received a phone call from him nor do I expect one. He will probably delegate it to someone who will protect their "golden boy" or "sweep it under the rug" making all of my effort useless. In order to avoid this happening again and to set an example they will likely terminate me thus ending any attempt to rid the man who they believe will save the company. Why can't I be seen by them as the one who will turn the company around and entrusted to do more to change it? Why can't they provide me with a chance to prove what it is I can do? Why should I even be concerned about this?

Why am I boring you with this?

Well, everyone has left the restaurant and I probably should also. Thank you again for listening, my Love, even if I went back on my promise to not speak to you about my job.

A12 MONTHS WITHOUT YOU   Part 1

8/24

Hello my Love,

I speak to you this evening on what should be a celebration, yet I don't feel in the mood to be happy. I was finally able to voice all of my concerns regarding the store manager to the HR manager, a conversation which lasted about 50 minutes in which I was able to do the majority of the talking while the gentleman listened and periodically asked me questions or to be more specific about a situation I mentioned. Saying I felt "satisfied" for what I had done feels inappropriate; instead I will say I'm "content" for someone finally willing to listen to me even though I resorted to having to directly contact the president of the company. Given my experience with the person in the same position at 'our' former employer, I wasn't looking forward to having to go this far to find some type of resolution.

    I heard a strategy several years ago which has helped me during phone conversations with people in a higher position than my own, which happens to be all of them: make sure you are standing while speaking on the phone. It will make you feel confident as though you're addressing the person directly and you are both on the same level. I feel foolish I didn't do this during my conversations with the DM and allowed my intimidation of his position affect what I needed to tell him. But I won't completely blame myself for what occurred; he happened to catch me at a moment in which I was unprepared and he sounded as though he had an "arrogance" about who he was, making me feel as though I was a "bother" to him and unworthy of his time and attention. Although a device and distance separated us, he was still capable of reducing me to the size of an ant, a mindless working insect whose existence was devoted to laboring because of it doing what it was created to do.

I can't say the decision to communicate to the president was my idea – the credit goes to my elderly neighbor who lives across the street. During my previous visit after my final conversation with the DM, I told her of how powerless I felt and frustrated no one was willing to listen to what I knew was wrong. At one point, I made an "off-the-cuff" remark during his recent visit which the president told me to contact him if there was anything he could do for me and almost immediately my neighbor said, "Then why don't you tell him?" as if the solution was simple which it must have been for a 70-something-year-old woman. I hadn't planned on pushing the issue any further especially since my failed interaction with the DM felt like a "dead end," as though there was no one else I could turn to for assistance. I had to accept the store manager was too connected with upper management and, as I described to the HR manager, "untouchable." As for why none of my coworkers has said anything to him or made a report to the district HR representative, I informed him all of the other employees in the store are afraid of being "targeted" by the store manager either resulting in the transfer to another location or termination because he simply doesn't like them or doesn't want that employee to be on his staff at the new store when he, according to him, will be placed in charge of it next year. To me, it's a bold assumption to make, almost a "haughty" one considering several months ago the staff was told the store was closing and we would all have to reapply for our jobs and only being offered a position if we were fortunate to be on the store manager's "good side" rather than on our reputation with the company and our contributions to it. Yet there's this "golden boy" who is being protected by the right people and regarded as some type of "savior" who will single-handedly and immediately improve the firm overnight.

I had prepared a statement I was going to convey to the DM but he ended our conversation before I was able. Not wanting to "let it go to waste" I said it to the HR manager which is the following: 'If I decide to continue my career with this company and would someday hope to become a manager, is [store manager's name] the type of manager I need to aspire to become? Is he the type of manager the company wants in its stores?'.

I'm almost embarrassed to say this, but I can't recall ever using the words "b--ching a--" and other "colorful" language in a conversation with someone in corporate. But given the severity of the situation I felt as though it was appropriate. Taking a recent lesson I learned from my department manager, sometimes it's necessary to "season" a serious conversation with atypical words in order to get your point across and make sure the receiver is paying attention. Otherwise the information will "go in one ear and out of the other" just as how our former-assistant-department manager described his talks with the store manager regarding his reasons for leaving and his requests, if granted, would cause him to remain with the firm. And although I almost convinced myself I wouldn't say it, I summarized the reason for the store's low morale in a few words: 'He is a bad manager.' I even invited the HR manager to visit our location in the next two days to listen to how my coworkers feel under the promise of a confidentiality agreement in which the store manager wouldn't be informed of who said what, as I mentioned earlier, my Love, which would lead to the same fate as the store's recently-transferred co-manager or even worse. And the only reason I've stepped forward isn't because I had something against the man for reprimanding me or was attempting to advance my career – I wanted to do what was right for the loyal, hard-working, and dedicated people whom I regard as part of my family: both the employees and the customers.

Coincidentally, one of my coworkers is here this evening and I informed him of what I did earlier. He is one of the few who has suffered the most because of this manager and honestly I'm surprised he hasn't "lashed out" at him to the point I admire him for his restraint. Coworkers like him are why I did this and I sincerely hope something is done to improve the situation at the store.

Well, it's 15 minutes after their closing time and I should allow the staff here to do what is necessary so they can leave soon. Sorry I talked to you again about my job but I felt as though of all the people I know, you would understand and support what I did. And for that, it assures me what I did was right.

Thank you again, my Love.

A12 MONTHS WITHOUT YOU   Part 1

8/27

Hello my Love,

I had considered working a half an hour over my shift today in order to "round out" my end-of-the-week hours to 39, but after I returned from my meal I just wanted to get out of there as soon as I was able even if it meant at my scheduled end-of-shift time. I can't explain as to why I suddenly changed my mind; I was wanting to have some time to myself to write to you this evening even if it was only half an hour more.

While I was soaping the floor in the prep area, I looked over at my seafood counter and noticed a young, attractive woman standing in front of my case looking at the various items within it. As I routinely do, I stopped spraying the floor, walked through the swinging door separating the prep area from the sales floor, and approached the customer. When she turned her face toward me, I thought I had immediately recognized her features since, collectively, they were ones I had seen countless times. Although the woman's hair was blonde and her voice possessed a local "tinge" to it, I could have sworn the person in front of me, even with painted-red fingernails, was you. I eventually sold the customer a piece of salmon stuffed with a seafood mixture and made sure I attached a sticker containing the preparation instructions onto the cellophane wrap in order for her to cook it properly. I casually referred to the two bottles of wine I noticed in her cart, produced at a nearby vineyard, and informd her, 'Sometimes the vineyards themselves sometimes do sampling here at the store.' I even thought about commenting on the strawberry-rhubarb pie she also had in her cart which, aside from the salmon and the wine, were the only other items she had in there but I didn't want to appear nosy for analyzing her future purchases. Her eyes...I couldn't separate myself from them because they were the same color as yours. I typically don't look at anyone directly because of shame I always feel while working there but looking at her was the closest I've felt to looking at you that isn't a photograph, a fleeting memory, or a recreation in my dreams – this felt real. Not wanting to frighten her, I told her if she was brunette, she would look almost exactly like a good friend I haven't seen in three years. I had considered telling her the woman she resembled was someone whom I loved but I didn't want to make her feel uncomfortable. It was then time for me to "break down" the case for the evening and I did turn to look toward the other side of the store hoping she would return and perhaps invite me to her place to share the wine and maybe some of the dessert. Of course, as my luck has been for awhile, she didn't come back and I ended up "punching out" on time. Although my pants had a rip in them near my private area possibly exposing my underwear to the world, I didn't want to sacrifice the time to return to the house and change into a pair of "intact" pants when I could, instead, have more time to write to you and hopefully in 'our' booth which I'm fortunate to have seen it being cleared off upon my arrival. But before this, I was in the parking lot and removed this notebook from the passenger's seat as I typically do, by opening the door, where it's located rather than taking it with me when I exit from the driver's side. After having shut the door, I realized I hadn't checked my phone since my "meal" earlier and must have not looked at it as I typically do before I leave the store. Assuming no one had contacted me, I reluctantly decided to go ahead and check to see if my sister, father, or a telemarketer had attempted to contact me. I discovered no one had called (unusual but typical) but there was a text message. I assumed it was probably another unintentional one from the former pharmacy where I no longer receive my medication and was pleasantly and happily surprised to discover it was from you.

    I can't express how often I have awaited that moment, one I concluded would never happen again because I accepted, from your silence, you probably had forgotten about me, in your mind I didn't exist, and arrived at a point in your life in which I could nor should be involved in it. I was just a memory fading away the older you became and someone you may recall occasionally in your dreams who had no purpose for a married woman.

    But here I am, seated in *A12*, wondering how to respond to you as I stare at your photo, two sheets of the laminated corners bent and separating from each other from the numerous times it has been tucked into the top-left corner of each page onto which I write, the pocket on the inside of this folder from the frequency of my removing and replacing your photo into it, and of course how often I've placed 'you' in the pockets of my clothing so if someone does take this notebook I would still have your smiling at me while I write. I realize I could make another copy, rewrite your words on the back of it, and then laminate it so it appears brand new but this particular one has been with me since I made it about four years ago. Your eyes have watched me record my thoughts, feelings, worries, concerns, ideas, and observations. You kept me company while I sat alone in the office for hours during those months and then later kept me motivated to succeed at my job at another firm from your place tucked in the buttons of my keyboard. And yesterday on my day off while working outside on my model kit, 'you' were held in a hobby vise I use to hold pieces which had adhesive applied to them and wait for the bond to hold.

Looking at you now, I know how I have to respond to your inquiry: the way I should have been to you over five years ago.

The reason I tell you these things is because whenever I return to the house at night and drive down one of the main roads intersecting the street on which I reside, I wonder if what it is in my notebook will be the final words I will ever write, the last letter written to you under the impression there won't be another. I think to myself you will never be able to hear me read the sentences to you nor will they ever be seen by your beautiful eyes and instead end up in a box tucked away at my parents' house or thrown away. But just in case the horrific happens tonight and either a family member or stranger finds this among the debris and my corpse, please know I've thought about you every day since 'our' last encounter three years ago. You have been in my mind, my dreams, and especially my heart even when I was at my most depressed and hopeless. You gave me strength, determination, and direction, my Love, and for that alone I am indebted to you. You believed in me when no one else would, realized I saw the world unlike everyone, and was loved by at least one woman during my brief existence. I cannot express my deepest gratitude to you adequately in words so please realize it is immense and immeasurable. If you want to know how many times you were thought of by me, look up at the stars on a clear night. Each one also represents a wish I made for you to someday reappear in my life. Tonight if I make it to the house safely, I will thank the stars rather than make a request to them. They deserve my appreciation, and above all else, to the Lord Himself, I am thankful.

Well, my Love, my pants need to be repaired before my next shift begins in about 11 and a half hours and I want to be able to awake before it and give my thanks to God for bestowing a wonderful gift onto me this evening. It's the right thing to do for His blessing.

Thank you again for listening, my Love, and for making this day special for me, even if you aren't here with me in person. It's close enough.

PAUL S. DOIZÉ

To be continued in Part 2

About the Author

Paul S. Doizé was born in Georgia in 1981. Because of his father's employer, he spent his childhood and adolescence living in cities throughout the mid and southern parts of the United States. Two weeks after his high school graduation, he began working for a local grocery retailer and remained with the company in order to help fund his college education. In 2007, he graduated with a bachelor's degree in business administration and a minor in English from the University of North Carolina at Greensboro. He currently resides in North Carolina.

www.ingramcontent.com/pod-product-compliance
Lightning Source LLC
Chambersburg PA
CBHW020421010526
44118CB00010B/365